Noonan's Ex

Lake Winnapausakee, NH

Newport, RI

New York City

Grand Haven, MI

Lansing, MI

Chicago IL

South Bend, IN

Kankakee, IL

Columbus, OH

, KN

St. Louis, MO

so, OK
Patriot
Club

Knoxville, TN

dquarters,
rings, OK

Chattanooga, TN

Port St. Lucie, FL

Palm Beach Gardens, FL

Early Years

Middle Period

Latter Period

A PATRIOT'S CALLING

Living Life Between Fear and Faith

MAJOR DAN "NOONAN" ROONEY

A Patriot's Calling
Copyright 2012 by Dan Rooney

Paperback ISBN 978-1-936750-83-2
Hardcover ISBN 978-1-936750-91-7
eISBN 978-1-936750-89-4

Published by Yorkshire Publishing
6271 E. 120th Court
Tulsa, OK 74134

Text Design: Lisa Simpson
www.SimpsonProductions.net

DEDICATION

To Jacqy, the love of my life. To Mom and Dad. To my girls, who teach me something every day. To all the spirit warriors who have shown me the way.

FOLDS *of* **HONOR**
Major Dan "Noonan" Rooney

FOREWORD

JIM NANTZ — CBS SPORTS COMMENTATOR

As a sports commentator for CBS, I have many opportunities to be involved with great people and organizations dedicated to helping others. In June of 2007, I received an email and opened it without expectation. What I encountered was an eloquent and heartfelt account of sacrifice, honor, and dedication. What I read was a story. A story of two brothers dedicated to keeping a promise, made months prior in a time of chaos and fear, to never leave the other behind. And the story of a man, unknown to me at the time, who would carry on this promise for all American soldiers in harms way. He would be their brother, their fellow soldier, and keep their legacy alive.

Major Dan Rooney is a husband, a father, and now my friend. Dan gathers his inspiration from the people he encounters in life. His is genuinely interested and invested in their dreams and passions while unknowingly inspiring others. On that day in June, Major Rooney inspired me. He humbly asked for my assistance and in return I was given the opportunity to serve others through a game I have loved throughout my life. Like so many of us fortunate to play golf, Dan grew up with a deep love for the game and the character it builds.

Major Dan "Noonan" Rooney is not only a PGA golf professional but also an F-16 fighter pilot; his call-sign originating from Danny Noonan in the movie Caddyshack. He is not what you imagine as the typical fighter jock. His self-depricating humor is genuine and endearing. Noonan is the first one to tell you he is an ordinary guy with an extraordinary calling. He will tell you there is no such thing as chance. Life is made up of encounters that guide us on our unique path. The ultimate reward is the fulfillment that comes from following your destined path.

When Major Dan asked me to believe in his big dream, a concept called Patriot Golf Day, I told him that I was honored to stand by him. We started small, but I have watched it grow into a band of brothers spanning this great Nation. With his leadership and passion, I know this noble mission will continue to grow and change lives for generations to come.

As a broadcaster, I have witnessed my share of "amazing stories" in living color. The drama of sport, competition, and life. The defining moments that make it all so compelling and give us hope. Major Dan's story is one of the best I have ever been blessed to witness. *A Patriot's Calling* is about living life between fear and faith. The stories that Major Dan shares are inspiring and empowering. They push us to the edges of life. They remind us that we are called to use our time and talents to positively impact the world. He allows us to climb into his cockpit and takes us on a journey. A journey marked by success, failure, laughter, and tears. He shares the stories of many remarkable people and the ways they have prepared him for the mission of living. We can all learn from the lessons of Major Dan's life.

Major Dan will tell you he has been blessed, but we are the ones who have been blessed to know him. He is a uniter of people, a difference-maker and one of the greatest patriots I have ever met. I know you will enjoy reading his fascinating story. You will feel in the end as I do now, he is an American treasure and someone we should be proud to call our friend.

—Jim Nantz

CONTENTS

PROLOGUE

QUINTESSENCE

The way to see by faith is to shut the eye of reason.

—BENJAMIN FRANKLIN

As I sat on the dark rooftop of the 332d Fighter Squadron, the harsh smell of the burn pits was a constant reminder of the war we were fighting in Iraq. I was enveloped by searing heat and screaming jet noise. Dust particles permeating the air made the white, blue, and green lights of the runways shimmer. As I watched the afterburner of an F-16 taking off, I noticed the twilight glow on the eastern horizon as the sun struggled to bring light to the darkness of war. I thought about my family and the irony of the same peaceful sun setting in Oklahoma a few hours earlier. In that moment of reflection my thoughts drifted. Reaching across to the pocket on the left arm of my desert-brown flight suit, I pulled out a pencil and curiously jotted down the word *quintessence*.

The great philosopher Aristotle discovered quintessence. He dubbed it the fifth element, the soul and essence that breathed life into the four elements of earth, air, fire, and water. Quintessence is the ultimate, the core, the epitome, and, indeed, the very marrow of our lives. We each have a true essence; the purpose of life is to discover it.

I do not believe in chance or coincidence, rather the force of synchronicity. Synchronicity—*chance with a purpose*—is all around us; those instances recognize our encounters with synchronicity. The forces of synchronicity are like sign-posts on the road of life directing us toward our quintessence. Each time we acknowledge the presence of synchronicity, our faith becomes stronger and our fears weaken.

Lost in the reflective recesses between F-16 combat sorties in support of Operation Iraqi Freedom, I felt a calling from God to share the miraculous fusion of people and experiences uniquely placed in my life. As I channeled my thoughts into higher resolution through the keys of my sandblasted laptop, I began to understand my journey toward quintessence and recognize how the forces of synchronicity had shaped my life.

Deployed to Iraq as a member of the 332d Fighter Squadron.

NOONAN'S TRAVELS

★

In *A Patriot's Calling* we will travel many places. I wanted to include these maps as a guide.

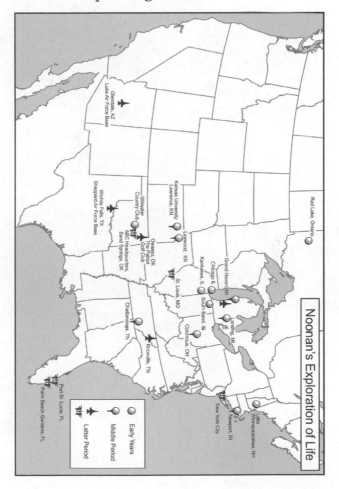

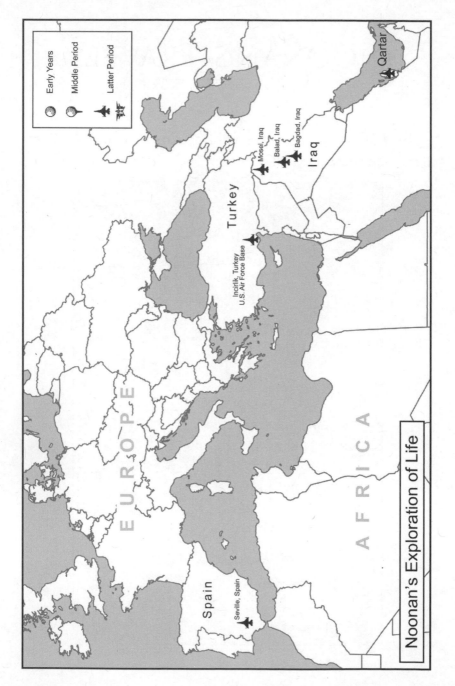

Noonan's Exploration of Life

1.

I AM

Your options are limited only by your fears.

—UNKNOWN

My mom and dad dedicated their lives to shaping my sisters and me into people who paid attention to the forces guiding our lives preparing us for the pursuit of quintessence.

Dad, a professor, spent four decades teaching and mentoring thousands of students. Each semester a new batch of undergraduates would take their seats in old dingy, classroom 101 at Oklahoma State University for *The Geography of Sport.* On Rooney standard time, five minutes late, a fiery Irishman wearing Ray-Ban Wayfarers catapulted through the door, and the students quickly began to realize that this would be like no other class they had ever taken.

If GQ magazine had a distinguished-professor edition, Dad would have graced its cover by now. Decked out in his tweed jacket with suede elbow pads and a maroon and yellow striped tie with a Windsor knot, he welcomed the next generation of young leaders to his laboratory. Dad is a passionate teacher and truly cares about his students. In a savant-like fashion he remembers nearly every one of them as well as their hometowns.

My sisters and I were the luckiest students on earth. Though we did not get our degrees from Oklahoma State, we are permanently enrolled in Dr. Rooney's classroom of life. One of Dad's core beliefs is that you have to travel in order to fully understand the world. Every June, as we would back out of our dusty gravel driveway bound for places unknown, he would remind us in his raspy voice, "Kids, don't go to sleep or you'll miss the most important part. Your experiences write the amazing book titled, 'Your Life.'"

When I was ten, my parents took us to Europe. We traveled with a worn-out copy of *Europe on 25 Dollars a Day*. We were humble and hungry students spending two months touring and soaking up European culture and history. But the most impactful part of the trip for me was the opportunity of flying on a Boeing 747 Jumbo Jet.

I remember gazing out the terminal window and witnessing the most beautiful bird I had ever seen. "PAN AM" emblazoned on her side, she stood six stories tall. I was awestruck by the sheer might of the machine. As I walked down the jet bridge, my excitement grew. To this day the distinctive smell of a jet bridge triggers an emotional mixture of adventure and possibility. As I boarded the plane, I touched her skin for good luck and was greeted by the luckiest man on earth—the pilot. To a little guy, he had the aura of a superhero. I gave him a firm handshake, a handshake with reverence.

Walking down the aisle, full of inspiration, I knew at age 10 that I was going to be a pilot. As I climbed into my psychedelic blue and yellow paisley-patterned seat, I passionately announced to a couple of blue hairs snacking on dried prunes in the seats next to me that someday I would be a pilot. "Sure you will," came their response along with a very patronizing pat on the head.

That part of life has never changed. I figured out early on that most people will not encourage or understand the passion that burns within your soul, so the key is not to rely on external influences in life for motivation or affirmation. That fire burning in your soul is quintessence. Embrace life and stride bravely toward your passions. The pursuit is what makes us feel alive. You are the only one who understands who *"I am."*

I am a runt kid who grew up in the dust bowl of Stillwater, Oklahoma. I was an ordinary boy with an extraordinary calling. Nothing came easy, but Mom and Dad always reminded me that we are all here for a reason. "Son, no one like you has come before, and no one with your gifts will come again. It is up to you to figure out what your calling is in life."

I internalized my parents' core belief that life is not a dress rehearsal and committed my life to creating my own reality. As a young man I dreamed of the ultimate job description. I was determined to live a life of faith and not one limited by fear. My childhood dreams would become a reality. I have been blessed to fly faster than the speed of sound and create a foundation to help military families, all while getting to be involved every day with the game I love.

I am first and foremost a husband and the grateful father of four girls. I was a slightly above-average student at the University of Kansas, where I earned a bachelor's in geography and a master's in sports psychology.

My life's greatest honor is fighting for freedom alongside a heroic band of brothers. While flying an F-16 fighter jet as a major in the Oklahoma Air National Guard, I have logged three tours of duty in Iraq. I have slipped from beneath life's narrow and limiting canopy of safety.

My office.

As a PGA golf professional I have toured the country and witnessed acts of skill and dedication performed by a most professional and extraordinarily philanthropic group of people.

In a traditional sense I am not qualified to provide counsel on the pursuit of your quintessence or the forces of synchronicity. I doubt many spiritual gurus or self-help experts have been profoundly influenced by movies such as *Caddyshack*,

Top Gun, Dead Poets Society, and *Field of Dreams.* You may want to stop reading here when I tell you these movies have significantly altered my life.

The most important lesson that I have learned is that I am capable of change. Armed with this power, our lives have no limits. We are evolving with each breath. We are capable of becoming or doing anything. I have learned over time to harness the infinite energy of each moment in pursuit of my essence. To love each day. Faith has given me the courage to relinquish control and the gift of freedom that comes from letting go. I have grown to understand and accept that my greatest blessing is also my greatest curse. I internalize my emotions and other people's emotions, good and bad, at the deepest levels.

Quintessence is elusive. It's God's reward to those who push themselves physically, spiritually, and emotionally. This triad is the elixir of life, and each day I strive to make a little progress in these three areas. Discovering quintessence is a lot harder than becoming the best that we can be. Being the best at anything involves setting high goals and doing what is necessary to attain them. Deciding what we want in life, crafting a plan to get there, and executing that plan are all parts of attaining success. While these skills are important, the world is littered with successful people who have failed to find their quintessence. Realizing our quintessence demands that we go much deeper. Becoming a pure and concentrated essence of ourselves, the perfect embodiment of one's self, is a daunting task. God put each of us here for a reason. Fulfillment is discovering that reason. As we move closer to our essence, the wave of life's energy intensifies. We all have experienced quintessence in fleeting moments of pure peace and happiness that visit us now and then. Everything seems right, and our energy is limitless. These brief, perfect experiences stun us with their power but too often vanish into the chaos. They leave us wanting more, and so inspired, we strive on. We continue the passionate journey in pursuit of quintessence. In so doing we become better persons—physically, spiritually, and emotionally.

We all have a calling in life. The universe uses synchronicity to point us toward our intended path. Along our travels, people and experiences are placed in our lives to test us. To transform us. To guide us. To shed light on what really matters. You will meet many of the people responsible for pointing me in the right direction in the pages to come. These spirit warriors, as I call them, have helped me develop a set of maxims that I try and live by each day.

I begin each morning with a quick prayer for an open heart and an open mind. I pray that I will have the courage to pursue the world's infinite gifts. The courage to embrace the people and circumstances that will severely test me along my path. The courage to recognize and learn from the moments of synchronicity in life.

Today is the greatest day of my life. Whether it brings success or setback, pleasure or pain, I continue to learn from the experiences and spirit warriors on my journey. Synchronicity has placed them in my life. It's through their confluence that my essence is illuminated and my life has been altered in unimaginable ways.

In the end it is pretty simple: we want to be happy. To find happiness in life, we need more faith and less fear. When we trust in God, we will be rewarded. Faith is a prerequisite to overcome the fears that stand between us and quintessence. While some of my days are better than others, my commitment never wavers.

This is my path...

2.

UNITED 664

★

Freedom is not free.

—U.S. MILITARY

Although I live in Oklahoma, I spend time during the summer in Michigan. Grand Haven, home to the Rooney family golf club, is an idyllic lakeside community on the eastern shore of Lake Michigan. The homes, constructed of traditional white clapboard, are each fastidiously painted. Traditional values and American flags proudly waving conspire to produce a living yet ageless photograph circa 1940.

Life moves at a Norman Rockwell pace in Grand Haven. The evenings are my favorite times. Infused with the glow of a perfect sunset, the boardwalk comes alive with families and friends tending to ice cream cones. The engaging sounds of conversation and abundant laughter spill generously from open windows and are carried on the warm lakeshore breeze.

It was on a routine trip back to Grand Haven, the bastion of serenity, that I would be shaken to the core. My life was about to take a dramatic turn.

In early June, 2006, I was headed back to Michigan to get some work done at the Grand Haven Golf Club. My usual route takes me by plane through Chicago and into Grand Rapids, followed by a short drive into Grand Haven. Anyone who travels through that part of the country knows that weather delays are nothing out of the ordinary. Finally it was time to board United Flight 664 bound for Grand Rapids.

As I boarded the plane, I stole a glance inside the cockpit and marveled at the thousands of lights and switches. Performing this same act as a young boy had sparked my fascination with flying. You never know when a moment of synchronicity will be the trigger for the next significant change in your life.

As I turned right I walked by a young soldier in dress greens sitting quietly in first class. *Probably home on leave,* I thought, making my way through the cabin. *It's nice to see that someone has taken care of this young corporal.* After settling into my coach seat I stared out the window and took in the show of lights outside. I have always loved airports at night—there is something truly awesome about them all.

A few micro-sleeps later the engines roared to life as we finally took off. We climbed out of the Windy City, and I leaned over to admire the John Hancock building peering mystically through the clouds.

The flight was short and turbulent. We were up and down in 20 minutes. These flights are particularly busy for pilots. As we bounced around the sky, I reminisced about how fast our T-38 Talon training flights were as we would hop across the desolate plains of Texas out of Sheppard Air Force Base. The T-38 is a two-seat supersonic trainer the Air Force uses to shape the next generation of fighter pilots. During our instrument sorties, by the time you reached 25,000 feet you were running your checklist for the descent, which typically started 50-plus miles away. In the T-38 instrument phase we learned how to fly in the clouds and at night with our instruments as our only guide. It was the first experience of learning how to think at 500 miles per hour, a skill that was honed, but ultimately you had it in your DNA or you didn't. The T-38 instrument phase is where most wannabe fighter pilots wash out...

"BING!"

The chime of the seatbelt sign interrupted my trip down nostalgia lane as United 664 descended into Grand Rapids just before midnight. While I always remain open to the infinite possibilities that come with every journey, landing in Grand Rapids kicked off a succession of events that would permanently alter my life's course. As we taxied to the gate, the captain came over the speaker and made an announcement: "We have an American hero on board with us tonight."

My thoughts immediately shifted to the soldier sitting in first class. *What had he done?*

After a long pause the captain continued, "We are carrying the remains of Army Corporal Brock Bucklin...and his twin brother, Corporal Brad Bucklin, has brought him home from Iraq."

My heart sank. My life and my values came suddenly rushing to the surface. I had recently returned home from a tour of duty in Iraq thinking that I had left the death and destruction of the war behind. Tonight I realized I was wrong. It had followed me home.

The captain went on to make a request. He asked everyone to please remain seated as a sign of respect until Brock Bucklin's remains were removed from the aircraft. This was the least we could do as Americans to honor this young man and his family, who had given everything for our country. For the next 30 minutes I watched over the right side of the plane as this hero's ceremony unfolded before my eyes. The images enveloping the scene and the lives of the Bucklins were forever burned into my soul.

The flash of emergency vehicles broke the night. It had been raining earlier, and though the drizzle had already stopped, the tears continued to fall, their gleam visible with every breach of blue light. The Bucklin family stood on the tarmac, holding each other, holding themselves, for warmth, as a shield against the pain. And then it came, conveyed from the belly of our 737, wrapped in a finely pressed, carefully placed five-by-nine swath of red, white, and blue by way of Dover Air Force Base—the meaning of sacrifice.

As Brock Bucklin's flag-draped casket descended the cargo hold ramp, inch by final inch, his four-year-old son Jacob, securely enveloped in the arms of his grandmother, could only watch, eyes fixed on the casket of his father, who would never hold him again. Brock had given up that treasure, his very life, for the sake of every other father and son, in the name of the colors that now covered his body, his world all gone, so the rest of us can live free.

The dignified hands of the honor guard, sheathed in brilliant white gloves that shone in the darkness, were raised in honor over the brave warrior's remains. With them, the ungloved hands of Brad Bucklin, now on the tarmac from his first-class seat, worked among them, gripping the remains of his brother's casket in intimacy, fulfilling the pledge they had made. Brock had come home for the last time.

As an F-16 pilot, I have encountered death and destruction in combat. I have seen the horrors of war firsthand. But until that moment I had never witnessed such anguish or experienced death in such a personal way. I was now seeing the other side of war. The true burden our military families have to bear was on full and sobering display, eliciting feelings of deep sadness and a tremendous sense of honor and respect.

Death. It is a reality. We are all going there some day. A place where we can no longer hold or be held by the ones we love on this earth. It's a place Brock Bucklin ventured to ensure that we have the freedom to spend each second on this earth as we choose knowing the day will come when we don't have any more time.

As I watched the Bucklin family facing such grief I couldn't help but wonder: *What if the tide of war turned on my family? What would their future be like without me?* I thought of the relationship I share with my dad and how important he is in my life. My eyes went back to the child on the tarmac, the four-year-old who was facing a lifetime without his father. I knew that Jacob and thousands like him, with their whole

27

lives in front of them, would have to grow up and face life without a parent to nurture them.

I became so engulfed in watching and pondering the gut-wrenching homecoming of Corporal Brock Bucklin on the tarmac that I hadn't paid any attention to what was taking place around me. When I finally turned away from my seat I was sickened by what I discovered. Many of the other passengers aboard United 664 had gotten off. They had ignored the captain's request to remain seated as a sign of respect. There were no connecting flights, there was no place else to go…except to crawl under the warm blanket of freedom we all sleep under each night as a result of sacrifices made by people such as Brock Bucklin and his family.

Anger like I had never felt before welled up inside of me. But I refused to believe that so many had deliberately turned their backs on Brock Bucklin. On his family. I knew in my heart that there must be patriots lying latent all over this nation. At that moment I felt a powerful force calling me to action.

Walking off the plane and up the jet bridge, I immediately called my wife Jacqy to share what I had just experienced. I told her that I had been given a mission in life and that I would need her support. As always, she readily and whole-heartedly agreed.

I didn't know exactly what I was going to do or where I was going to start, but I was certain of one thing as I walked through the dimly lit airport in Grand Rapids that night. I had to do something to help that family. I had not only to forgive but also to reach out to those people who had gotten off that plane and help them understand that freedom is not free. Though my path was unclear, something inside of me knew I had been preparing for this moment my whole life. God was calling me on a mission.

Corporal Brock Bucklin
was killed in Iraq on May 31, 2006.

PART ONE

★

OKIE

3.

OKIE

Act boldly and unseen forces
will come to your aid.

—DORTHEA BRANDE

M y parents, John and Sandy, are from Kankakee, Illinois, a manufacturing town about 50 minutes south of Chicago. They began their courtship in high school and continued dating as they went off to separate colleges. Dad attended the University of Illinois, where he was a member of the Sigma Chi fraternity. He then transferred to Illinois State, earning bachelor's and master's degrees in geography. Mom followed in my granddad's footsteps by going to Purdue University in Indiana. They married and headed for Worcester, Massachusetts, where Dad got a Ph.D. in geography from Clark University. He was what we call a fast-burner in the military, finishing his doctorate by his 25th birthday.

After brief stints at Wyoming, UCLA, Southern Illinois, and a year at the University of Exeter in Devon, England, Dad accepted a position as head of the new geography department at Oklahoma State University in 1969. He was the youngest person to hold the position at a major state institution. Driving a classic 912 Porsche at that time, Dad was dubbed by his father, "The Joe Namath of geography."

With a plan to eventually move back to the upper Midwest, my parents expected to stay in Stillwater for about five years. They are still there 40 years later.

Daniel J. Rooney was born on a brilliant, clear day in December of 1972. It's safe to say that Dad was excited; he had finally gotten a boy. I have two amazing older sisters, and we're all four years apart. Beth and Kate are wonderful people whom I admire. They were instrumental influences in my formative years growing up. I love them both very much despite the incessant harassment I received from them as their little brother—although I probably deserved most of it.

I will be forever thankful to my parents for raising me in a stable and loving home. They led by example. Both were physically, emotionally, and spiritually balanced. They instilled in me a set of guiding maxims that have endured throughout my life. This impenetrable foundation has given me the faith, courage, and persistence to pursue my dreams and see them through life's inevitable obstacles.

My parents allowed me to believe in myself and always made me feel safe despite the innumerable risks and challenges that come with life. They were never overprotective and did not hesitate to let me fail. They did not intervene. Though it was hard for them to watch me experience failure they understood its inherent value. I knew that when I fell, they would be there to help me get back up. Courage is instilled in children through an unquestionable belief that their parents will always be there if they fail.

4.

MOM

✪

Pray as though everything depended on God.
Work as though everything depended on you.

—SAINT AUGUSTINE

Mom was a committed homemaker. While she was generous with her time, regularly volunteering at the church and hospice, family always came first for her. Mom was quick to make me feel special when I walked in from school. Signaling my arrival through the drawling creak of the screen door, I was often met with the aromatic pleasure of baking bread and a smile from Mom equally as warm. My dad, my sisters, and I never doubted for a second that we were the highest priority in her eyes. There was ample room in her heart for all of us. Mom made sure that we sat down at the dinner table together to discuss the events of the day.

A spiritual inspiration and a devout Catholic, Mom was the rock of the family, a pillar of strength. She dissected complex issues and was always there to talk through difficult times. But there were no free rides with Mom; she held everyone in the house accountable, teaching us discipline and integrity. To say that she was practical doesn't aptly cover it. Mom took that element to new heights. Her pragmatic approach, although I'm somewhat reluctant to admit it, has definitely rubbed off on me, serving me well over the years.

Mom clearly demonstrated the value of volunteerism and service. She taught me to embrace the world with unconditional love and kindness. She endowed me with a deep sense of faith and responsibility and explained that God gives you unique talents and calls you to use them. She taught me to combine daily prayer with preparedness. "If you prepare to the best of your abilities, everything else will be okay," she would say. "Try really hard, and then let go. Add *thy will be done* after every request because we don't really know what is best for us."

When I was seven, we were on a family road trip when I came down with a horrible stomachache. We pulled into a McDonald's. Dad took my sisters inside; Mom stayed in the car with me and put her hand on my stomach. She asked me to put my hand on hers and said, "For where two or more are gathered together in My Name I am there in the midst of them." She softly prayed aloud that I would feel better. Almost instantly I went from sweating and aching to feeling fine. As I ate my chicken nugget Happy Meal, thinking about what had just happened, I knew I would never again doubt God's presence.

First Communion
age 8.

36

5.

DAD
★

Success is peace of mind, which is a
direct result of knowing you did your best
to become the best that you are capable of becoming.

—JOHN WOODEN

Next to my wife, my dad is my best friend. He was the best man in my wedding and has always been a huge influence in my life. We have been working and playing golf together for years. While I was growing up, Dad played golf almost every day the weather permitted, and I remember how excited I got each evening when Dusty, our dog, would announce his homecoming.

Dusty, by the way, was one of the ugliest little dogs to ever roam the earth. But Dad comes from a long line of Irish storytellers, and before we knew it, we were no longer burdened with an ugly mutt. The tale of Dusty spread like the lore of the leprechaun. This vile canine had been transformed from a roadside mongrel into one of the rarest breeds on earth. It turned out that Dusty was actually a miniature

Egyptian wolfhound given to Dad as a gift from the mother of an eternally grateful exchange student from Egypt. With an average life expectancy exceeding 30 years, she was at that time one of only 63 remaining in the world. The breed was on the verge of extinction due to a recessive impotence gene. If you saw an Egyptian wolfhound, you would understand the impotence issue because you could believe that no living animal would want to breed with it. Dusty's drastic underbite, which protruded an astonishing two inches, was a cruel feat of nature's engineering that allowed her to ferret out rats from the deepest corners of the pyramids.

Upon Dad's arrival home, Dusty, who looked like a cross between a goat and a mangy rat scurrying across the kitchen floor, sounding the alarm. Words cannot describe what Dusty thought was a bark. I can only say this bloodcurdling noise emanated from somewhere deep in her bowel region.

She would be in her full barking glory by the time Dad would barrel up the driveway like Mario Andretti hitting the pits. I would run to the back door and hug his leg. I affectionately remember his natural cologne, a concoction of salty sweat and the Oklahoma outdoors mixed with a splash of gin and tonic.

I have many great memories of Dad from childhood. A vivid image lingers of him in his faded Cubbies hat with a whistle dangling around his neck. He was the neighborhood coach for us growing up, and he would often preach the hallowed sermons of Vince Lombardi while he ran us into the red dirt of Oklahoma: *"I firmly believe that any man's finest hour, the greatest fulfillment of all that he holds dear, is that moment when he has worked his heart out in a good cause and lies exhausted on the field of battle—victorious."* Though Dad quoted Lombardi with vigor, he had a much softer edge. When we would finish practice, Dad would load up the battle-worn gang for ice cream. We would head down to Braum's and sit with the windows down on those warm Oklahoma evenings, savoring the last sips of our chocolate sodas. Boys being boys. It was simple and good.

We shared lots of things. Golf and baseball were two of our favorites. I can still hear Dad's voice booming in concert with Harry Caray's over the airwaves, "Cubs win! Cubs win!" To this day the Chicago Cubs are a close second to the Catholic Church in my house. We still make the pilgrimage to catch a game at Wrigley Field almost every year. The weight of the world quickly melts when you're hanging with Dad in the Friendly Confines. Despite many painful losing seasons, Dad successfully passed the curse of being a Cubbies fan to me. I have already started taking my girls to the park, so I'm probably implanting the Cubs gene into their DNA, too.

Dad is one of the friendliest and most intelligent people I know. He has always been a pioneer, an innovator, and a big thinker. He is also a great natural athlete bestowed with the gift of speed. On a crisp fall evening in 1956 the crowd's cheers echoed down Kankakee's Main Street as a young redheaded halfback at Bishop McNamara High School took the ball 98 yards for a touchdown. To my knowledge that run still stands as the longest run in school history. No one but he realized it at the time, but looking back it's clear: Dad, like Forrest Gump, never stopped running.

In addition to being a distinguished professor, he's also an author, editor, publisher, sports consultant, and groundbreaking researcher. Dad's geographic analysis has opened new doors and permanently changed the way we view sports in this country. Dad literally wrote the book on *The Geography of American Sport*, the first to blend the two disciplines. He wrote and published six more in his career.

An incredible role model, Dad is directly responsible for empowering me with the courage to pursue quintessence and live in the realm between fear and faith. I only hope I can provide the same type of inspiration and guidance for my kids. Quite simply, Dad is my hero.

Dad instilled Patriotism at a young age.

6.

CADDYSHACK
★

Travel is fatal to prejudice,
bigotry, and narrow-mindedness.

—Mark Twain

With a profound understanding of the inner workings of the demographic and social aspects of geography, Dad, as I mentioned, believes that traveling the world is a critical component of a well-rounded individual and necessary to understand people. The people/place bond and the cultures you experience by crossing boundaries are invaluable.

I have fond memories of the Rooney summer expeditions. Every June we loaded up the big, dusty-brown Ford Econoline van, affectionately known as Norbert, and headed out on the great American road trip. We sang along to an eight-track of John Denver and logged in excess of 125,000 miles traveling country roads through 45 states. No movie players, no Walkmans, no communicative diversions at all. One of the big treats was making the occasional early pit-stop at a Holiday Inn Holidome. As we would walk in, we were greeted

41

with the overwhelming smell of swimming-pool chlorine, a harbinger of the hours of fun we were about to have.

The Rooneys were always up for a trip. Dad inherited much of his penchant for travel from Grandpa Rooney, who had a big heart, a great sense of humor, and a love for people. No matter where he was going, along the way at every gas station, restaurant, motel, and scenic wonder, my grandfather would talk to people about their lives, where they were from, their favorite teams—and always the weather. He asked lots of questions and listened to the answers. He truly had an open heart and an open mind. He was a lot like Will Rogers, a person he truly admired. Neither one of them ever met a man he didn't like.

We had many great adventures, but my favorite trips were to Lake Winnipesaukee in New Hampshire. Scenes from the classic *On Golden Pond* had been filmed at this picturesque lake, but it was our rustic accommodations there that made the experience so cool. The Grand Hotel at Lake Winnipesaukee was a classic New England-style lake house set on the shoreline. The weathered wooden floors, warped from years of great memories, would creak as we walked through the house.

I swear I grew gills those summers, always in the water. I even took my baths in the lake. I remember getting all soaped up and jumping off the second story of the Grand Hotel into the lake. It took some courage to take that leap. That space in time—hurtling toward the water—is the great sensation that exists in the realm between fear and faith.

Flying off the Grand Hotel at Lake Winnipesaukee.

The dawn at the lake was tranquil. We were up with the sunrise, greeted by the sounds of the lake gently lapping the shoreline. I have always enjoyed mornings and the prospects that each day brings. It's a chance to get a head start on the world. Every day a new beginning.

Our neighbor Frank had an old Chris-Craft boat. She was a wooden beauty made from the earth. An American icon, the stars and stripes waved from her stern. I felt like a young John Kennedy as we fired her up, heading for Wolfeboro to pick up the morning paper and an glazed old-fashioned donut. On the way home Frank would let me pilot the craft. As a youngster, to me it seemed like an eternity idling through the no-wake zone. But just like a thoroughbred when the gates open, I firewalled that wooden rocket as we passed the final buoy. The glassy water offered virtually no resistance as we glided across the lake. This was that first taste of intoxicating speed that in my adulthood would grow into a full-blown addiction.

I grew up on Lake Winnipesaukee; each summer was a coming of age. That summer I fell in love for the first time. She had California-blond hair, a perfectly tan body, and piercing ice-blue eyes. Her name was Lacey Underall. I met her on my neighbor Frank's Beta version of *Caddyshack*. I watched that movie so many times the tape frayed. I was 10 years old, and Lacey was my first love. I felt a strange, new, and exciting emotion, not too dissimilar to the euphoric feel of speed. My parents were not aware of my movie choice as I wouldn't have been allowed to watch it as a young, impressionable boy. I don't think it did any permanent damage. But as I reflect on my connections to *Caddyshack*, it gets a little scary. I grew up to be a PGA professional, and my wife looks a heck of a lot like Lacey...

7.

ADVERSITY

★

He who does not tire, tires adversity.

—MARTIN FARQUHAR TUPPER

Back in Oklahoma, my second home was on the golf course. As wonderful a place as Stillwater was to grow up in, there wasn't much else to do—in the eyes of a young boy, anyway. I know that I'm just one of thousands of kids all around the globe who have benefited from their association with golf, the greatest game on earth. It's so much more than chasing a little white ball and trying to get it into the hole. Golf was a huge part of my life growing up. It's also a critical component of who I am today and of how I have been able to contribute. There in the green classroom I found a path to quintessence. An avid and accomplished player, Dad carries a six-handicap. He set the love of the game in motion for me. I was five when Dad started letting me tag along and play with him and his regular group. The rules were simple: I played from the ladies' tees, and I couldn't slow them down. I would pound that sawed-off Toney Penna five-wood down the fairway and run after it like Billy Mills.

For the uninitiated, Penna was a professional golfer and golf club designer, and Mills is the legendary Native American track star from the University of Kansas who won the 10,000 meter in the 1964 Olympics in one of the greatest upsets in Olympic history. Billy Mills is a great inspiration to me and an example that anything is possible if you commit fully. I never fell behind when I was playing golf with Dad.

Over the years I have learned many lessons on the golf course. One of the first occurred an early bright summer morning just after Mom had dropped me off for the opening day of junior golf. I was so excited; Dad had taken the time to cut down a five-wood, five-iron, wedge, and putter for me. I had stayed up late the night before cleaning and polishing those clubs, getting ready for the big day. Arriving at the course the next morning, I was ecstatic. Every glistening drop of dew on the untouched surface of the course called out to me, inviting me to play. I nearly jumped out of the car before it came to a stop. Grabbing my clubs, I told Mom that I loved her and proudly hurried off toward the golf shop.

There was a big group of kids standing outside, lathering up with sunscreen. *A nice turnout*, I thought as I approached the building. Walking closer, I noticed a few of the kids elbowing each other and pointing in my direction. It took me a moment to realize it, but they were making fun of me. By the time I had reached the pack, they were howling with laughter. They were decked out with shiny new bags and the latest junior golf clubs. I was carrying four sawed-off clubs with no golf bag and two mud-stained golf balls. The welcoming feeling of the course, of the day itself, had turned to rejection and my excitement to shame. I quickly looked back for a possible retreat, but Mom had already gone. It was the first time that I had to stand alone and face adversity.

I remember that feeling of embarrassment and adversity like it was yesterday. The total isolation. It was a tough morning, but as with many times in my life, inspired by the wisdom of my parents, I turned an unpleasant situation into motivation; I took action. Strangely, this was my first sense of camaraderie with the game of golf. I realized that it wasn't the course that had turned on me. It wasn't nature. It wasn't the game. It was just some arrogant kids. The course, nature, the game, would all become my counsel. I was not the best golfer that day, but I was motivated to outwork every one of those kids. I never looked back and was beating them handily on the course for the next several years. It would be my first of many missions.

8.

COMPOUNDING INTEREST

✪

We are what we repeatedly do.
Excellence, then, is not an act but a habit.

—ARISTOTLE

Oklahoma summers can be Sahara hot. But they were pure heaven for me. There was nothing better than carrying my bag on a 100-plus degree day and feeling the crunch of burned-out Bermuda beneath my feet as I ambled down the fairway. Midway through the second 18, the fireball on the western horizon got downright repressive even for a sundog like me. I'd seek shelter and take a siesta under a blackjack oak tree. In most places, the blackjack would hardly qualify as a tree. But on the vertically challenged plains of Oklahoma it stands proudly. It looks like a hybrid between a tree and an armadillo and is one of the few species that can survive the state's repressively hot summers. While I was learning to play the game, these trees provided harsh and immediate feed-back as they spit my errant golf shots out with teeth marks.

Most days you could shoot a gun in any direction and not hit another living soul on the course. The buzz of locusts and a southerly zephyr rustling the trees were the only signs of life, other than a little runt of a kid with a sweat-stained hat chasing his ball. At that young age I observed that if you were willing to do things that others were not, you could make up a lot of ground on people with more talent.

Mark Twain once said, "I have never let schooling interfere with my education." While those words weren't referring to golf, they certainly apply to the game in my case. School has played a big role for me, but I have learned more about my essence on the links than I ever learned in the classroom.

By the time I was 11, my parents would routinely drop me off at the club first thing in the morning and pick me up at dusk. I had my clubs and a swimsuit, all that I needed to keep me occupied for the day.

I developed independence, social skills, problem-solving abilities, and sportsmanship during those summers on the course. In golf you are expected to call a penalty on yourself even if no one witnessed the infraction. Integrity is doing the right thing when no one is watching.

Golf also helped me develop a sound work ethic and taught me the value of a wage. My first job was working as a range rat for Dan Pryor, the local PGA professional, for $3.35 an hour. It was a great job, and I worked hard. I'd drive that rusty old range picker most every night. I looked like Charles Schultz's beloved "Pig-Pen" as I crisscrossed the range engulfed in a perpetual ball of dust. I was a frugal little guy and saved enough to purchase a car when I turned 16.

I learned a lot in that prefabricated metal cart barn. You would be amazed what golfers would leave behind in their carts. Let's just say a couple of Mrs. Murphy's menthol cigarettes, a wad of Mr. Anderson's Levi Garrett chewing tobacco, and a warm Coors Light provided a cheap but painful and highly effective lesson for one particular young man and went a long way in forever deterring him from future tobacco use.

Above all, golf gave me peace. The golf course was a safe place. My favorite times were on the golf course as a single, working on my game. On most days I was the first one there and the last one to leave. I was on a mission to get every minute out of the day.

Dad taught me the lesson about the awesome power of individual minutes compounded over time. "Son, the bet today is a $1 a hole, compounding." I replied "No problem" in a confident voice. What I did not realize but would soon understand were the mathematical implications. The first hole was worth $1...the second $2...the third $4...the fourth $8...the ninth $256...the fourteenth $8,192...the eighteenth...$131,072! "Dan, life is about getting a little better each day. Success doesn't happen quickly; rather, it's a result of a sustained effort over time." I listened to Dad and did my best to get the last few moments out of each day. I grew to understand that most days my progress would not be readily apparent and that true success comes through the compounding force of making a little progress every day.

By late September, summer's thermostat began to dial down giving way to a beautiful Oklahoma autumn. I had to hustle to the course after school to get in a round. Playing down the 18th hole at dusk, I remember walking through the cool pockets of air, often without enough light to see where the ball went. I developed a feel for it as I sensed the direction of the ball based on the strike rather than on sight.

The time passed quickly over the next several years and, like Dad, I became a pretty good golfer. I also managed to become a good student of life along the way. I had developed life skills and appreciations that would serve me well in the future. Most important, I begin to discover quintessence. Each hole played a role in helping me find my path. There is no team in golf; you are responsible for every shot. With each shot I gained insight into the great paradox of life—in the end it is you against you.

9.

FRITZIE

⭐

Our greatest glory is not in never falling,
but in rising every time we fall.

—CONFUCIUS

As my high school days were winding down and I was about to take off on my next journey, I was given one of the most meaningful opportunities of my life. While I wasn't aware of it at the time, I realize now that what I thought was just a shared adventure between a grandfather and a grandson was much more profound. I now know that it was all by design and that the person who gave me this gift knew exactly what he was doing.

My maternal grandfather, Phillip John Schriner, was a wonderful man, the consummate gentleman. Endearingly known to me as Fritzie, he completely embodied the spirit of living in the realm between fear and faith. He was an engineer, a conservationist, and an entrepreneur. Among his many accomplishments was creating fishing lures in his basement, a hobby that he grew into one of the biggest fishing-tackle companies in the world. His business took him all over

North America to test his fishing equipment and experience the great outdoors. One of his favorite spots was in Ontario, Canada, north of Red Lake. Fritzie chose this location as the backdrop to impart to me a lifetime of wisdom before I went off to college.

Fritzie picked me up at Midway Airport in Chicago in his Chevy Silverado. He had the truck all packed with gear, ready to go on our five-day fishing excursion. He threw me the keys, saying "Let's go enjoy life." A quick stop for some sliders at White Castle, and we were off.

Setting out on our journey, we savored our time together, just the two of us, listening to James Taylor, heading true north. We drove that day with the windows down and the scent of pines permeating the air. We were as thick as thieves without a worry in the world as we drove through the majestic Canadian countryside until the road literally came to an end. Highway 105 connects you to the town of Red Lake, but the only way north from there is by floatplane.

Looking back, I see the symbolism of this expedition. There we were, north of north, two guys, one 77 years old, nearing the end of life's road, and one 17 years young, getting ready to spread his wings. The significance of Fritzie situating me in an airplane to fly off into unknown territory cannot be overstated.

We spent the night in town, and in the morning we headed down to the slip. Arms overflowing with rods, reels, tackle boxes, food, and supplies, I felt the impulse to run to the plane like my daughters run from toy to toy. Reaching the water's edge, we advanced across the sun-bleached wooden planks of the dock to our water taxi. Our pilot, wearing a battered old sheepskin jacket, stuffed our gear into the yellow Norseman bush plane that lay still on the surface of the quiet morning lake amid the orange and violet light of the Canadian sunrise.

I scaled the three-rung ladder and climbed inside the tight quarters of the plane, where the pilot asked me to sit beside him in the right seat. I leapt into the copilot's chair and sat mesmerized, looking at all the gauges. By instinct the pilot, like a classic pianist, flipped a series of switches, turned knobs, and brought the engine rumbling and shaking to life. He slowly increased power, and the propeller whirled furiously. The floats rocked aft, and our nose rose above the spray, cutting through the glass surface of our liquid runway. As we picked up speed, I watched the pilot's hands gently pull back on the yoke. At his request, the nose rose higher, and at last the pontoons broke free from the clutches of the water. We climbed into the sky and deeper into the unknown.

Once airborne, the pilot turned the controls over to me. The first time I ever got to fly! My heart pounded as the adrenaline flooded my being. I couldn't wipe the smile off my face. I knew I was where I was born to be. The plane responded to every subtle turn of the yoke with another dose of life as it should be—limitless and free. Flying was certainly destined to be part of my quintessence.

For the next 30 minutes we soared over the virgin wilderness of Ontario, a sea of trees and cool stretches of blue shrouded in mist. I was completely present, free from the distractions of the world.

Upon landing, we skimmed across the surface of a secluded alcove and pulled up to the dock outside Sandy Beach Lodge. We gathered up all our supplies, piled out of the plane, and headed straight out for some fishing.

The silence of the morning was quickly interrupted by the unmistakable strike of a northern pike. My rod bending nearly 90 degrees, I embraced the battle. We were two fighters dueling on the water. Those fish were almost as competitive as Fritzie and I—but we got the best of them. Armed with the spoils of our victories, we found a little lunch cove, filleted some of our catch, and cooked it over an open fire. With bellies as full as our souls, we headed back out, chasing daylight.

Returning to base camp, we sauntered down from our cabin for dinner. As we walked into the smoke-stained lodge, we were met with the smell of meat and potatoes. We were so hungry we could almost taste the air. Animal skins and antlers adorned the walls of the outpost. We pulled up a couple chairs for dinner and traded stories with the other anglers.

Fritzie and me at Sandy Beach.

After finishing dinner, Fritzie broke out the cards for the traditional gin-rummy beating he was about to deliver to yours truly. But on this evening, as his weathered hands began to shuffle the cards, he motioned our host to bring over two cigars.

Fritzie looked me sharply in the eye as he precisely clipped the cigars before passing one over. It hit me: this was one of those monumental moments in life. It was a rite of passage. An initiation into the fraternity of manhood. Fritzie was still my grandfather, but we were now friends.

Fritzie was a competitive person and a cutthroat gin-rummy player. He never let me win. But I was warmly reminded that a man's true character comes through when he loses. Fritzie kept a running bet with everyone he played cards with. He would never collect, but you would be surprised how much debt you could accumulate over time playing gin rummy for a penny a point.

Fritzie kept the games lively. While I was usually the one being "schneidered," on that special night I managed to steal a few points from him. In the most loving way—that only someone from his generation could get away with—he said, "You son of a bitch. You got me with a shithouse," an outburst that brought our comrades at the lodge to a temporary silence but caused Fritzie and I to laugh so hard that there were tears running down our faces.

What with playing cards, fishing, and enjoying each other's company, we had lots of time to talk about life. He made it clear to me that he treasured our time together and cherished the opportunity to help me prepare for the world of adventures that lay ahead.

It's easy to see where Mom picked up her exemplary penchant for service that continues to trickle down through the generations. Born in Kankakee, Illinois, in 1912, Fritzie committed his life to serving the community. It all began when he took a summer job installing the first sewer system in West Kankakee; it spawned an overriding interest in community works projects. Fueled by this newfound passion, Fritzie became the first in his family to go to college.

The road was not always smooth for Fritzie. He told me about his rough start at Purdue. An outstanding football player dubbed the "Kankakee Express," Fritzie had visions of a big-time collegiate career of athletics. In fact, he was so focused on this dream that he almost flunked out his freshman year.

In life, what may appear as a tragedy in the moment often becomes a blessing. The famous country singer Garth Brooks, who hung around my dad's geography department at Okie State, said it best in a line in one of his songs, "Thank God for Unanswered Prayers." Toward the end of his freshman year Fritzie broke his shoulder playing football, causing him to call an audible. He shifted gears, concentrated on his studies, and received his degree. Reflecting on this message would help keep me between the lines during my time at the University of Kansas.

Fritzie's spirit of perseverance was an integral part of his character. He had no *quit* in him. When things didn't go as planned, he would keep fighting no matter what. He would adapt when needed, but he never gave up. Following World War II, he teamed up with his brother-in-law Harold LeMaster to form the L&S Bait Company. Their reach stretched globally as they sold lures around the world. Fritzie had most of his fishing-lure competitors "schneidered" for years. As the business became more competitive, Fritzie took the success of his manufacturing techniques and products and called another audible, launching into a new venue. The Kankakee Molding Company specialized in plastic-covered bolts that were used all over the United States. He reminded me, "There's always a way."

One afternoon during our Canadian adventure we encountered the mother of all squall lines. It rained so hard that we could barely see each other across the small boat. Soon our little craft was filling with water. We were miles from base camp and in danger of sinking. Frantically we started bailing water, and when one bucket wasn't enough to lower the level, we used our boots. In the middle of the Canadian wilderness, bailing with all our might, we laughed so hysterically we nearly fell out of the boat. Thankfully, our Boston Whaler was no *Titanic*, and we eventually purged the boat of enough water to keep ourselves afloat.

As we headed back to camp that night, Fritzie reminded me that the weather, like life, is unpredictable. "I hope your life is blessed with mostly fair skies, but you will encounter stormy periods and be tested. The most successful people in life spend 95 percent of their time failing. It's how you handle those failures that will determine your success in life. They are a vital part in your evolution. Embrace your struggles and understand that you are supposed to learn from them." I have certainly encountered some squalls in the last 20 years, but Fritzie would be proud that I have never hesitated to evaluate, embrace, and most importantly, take off my boots and bail.

As much as he was able to accomplish in life, Fritzie made sure to tell me to focus on life outside of work. He suggested that I ease off the throttle once in a while. I'll admit that this is not the easiest thing to do, but it's been an invaluable lesson.

Fritzie had an ability to appreciate where he was and who was with him. He was loyal, he was true, and he was a great teacher of family values long before the phrase was fashionable. He taught by example, often with a cutting sense of humor but always with a clearly defined objective. He was a great leader, someone who could give people constructive advice without causing resentment.

After a long and fulfilling journey, Fritzie died in Kankakee on October 7, 2004, at age 92, just a few blocks from the river that he so loved and the house where he had been born.

Fritzie's outlook on and zest for life have been a major source of motivation along my path and a driving factor in my recognition of the importance of community and service. Not a day goes by that I don't think of Fritzie. His legacy has shaped me for life. He is part of my quintessence. Oh, and for the record—the final tally of our gin-rummy bet is a little over $8,600. I will settle up over a cigar the next time we play gin.

10.

THE BLAST FURNACE

★

Faith consists in believing when it is
beyond the power of reason to believe.

—VOLTAIRE

I graduated from Stillwater High School in May of '91. My parents have given my sisters and me many things over the years, but their single greatest gift came in the form of a college education. Mom and Dad agreed to pay for school, but there was one stipulation: we had to leave the nest. They wanted us to get out of Oklahoma and experience life, to begin anew. Both of my sisters chose Catholic schools, one graduating from Notre Dame in South Bend, Indiana, and the other from Creighton University in Omaha, Nebraska. I opted for a public institution, the University of Kansas in Lawrence.

On August 6, 1991, I put the accelerator to the floor of my blue Honda Prelude and merged off of Highway 51 onto Interstate 35, chasing quintessence. As I turned north toward KU, I felt a feeling of both exhilaration and apprehension—that thrilling mixture of fear and faith. I knew only one person where I was headed: Ross Randall, the golf coach. Fresh from my trip with Fritzie, I was ready to embrace life's next chapter.

By the end of my first day I had 38 Sigma Chi pledge brothers and quickly realized the wonder of a new beginning. Fritzie and my parents were wise, and I will always cherish the opportunity I had been given to go out and face the world with no preconceived notions or expectations of who Dan Rooney was supposed to be. For me, going away to college was a *tabula rasa*—a clean slate.

Golf remained my central focus during freshman year. I was invited as a walk-on, so I had a place on the team, but it was vital that I continued to work diligently on my game. I devoted thousands of hours to honing my skills. The work ethic that I had developed through golf as a young boy is part of my quintessence. I think Coach Randall would attest to that.

In the summers I headed back to Stillwater to further develop my game. Without the interference of classwork, I could dedicate every day to pushing myself. I would head out on those blistering 100-plus degree days with a big cooler of water and shag my own golf balls in a field for 10 hours. I could have gone to the driving range, but I wanted to be accountable for every shot.

Wearing a hat and shorts but no shirt, I cooked in the heat. I prepared my hands for the assault by wrapping them with gauze and tape to prevent bleeding. There are no short-cuts to success. Most would find my routine miserable, but I relished the solitude and the battle against nature's blast furnace. There were days that my body would beg to stop, but my spirit would refuse. My only company was the occasional dust devil and the heat waves shimmering on the horizon. At the end of the day I was marred, drenched with sweat, and wearing a coat of fine red Oklahoma dust from hundreds of divots. At night I would go home to ingest Advil and soak my hands to prepare for the next day's battle.

In time I became one of the top players at the University of Kansas and earned a golf scholarship. Through sheer will and determination I passed many players who had much more raw talent than me. As I had been on that first day of junior golf several years earlier, I was motivated and willing to outwork anyone. I made every minute count.

Playing the 100th U.S.
Amateur at Newport.

11.

BALANCE

The first step is to fill your life with a positive faith
that will help you through anything.
The second is to begin where you are.

—NORMAN VINCENT PEALE

Through my determination to succeed in golf I learned a lot about myself. For starters, I learned that I have a tendency to become one-dimensional in my pursuit of something. As a result, my first two years at Kansas I drifted from my quintessence. I thought golf was the most important aspect of my life and believed it would ultimately be my future. While this would turn out to be partially true, it would not manifest itself in the way I had envisioned.

As is typical for any young man trying to find his way, I had lots of ups and downs, on and off the golf course. I developed a common and dangerous mindset: my self-worth and happiness were tied directly to my performance on the golf course. If my scores were good, I was happy. If my scores were bad, I was miserable. My ego was driven by fear.

65

My identity became Dan Rooney the golfer, not Dan Rooney the whole person. This is not only common in golf but is also a very prevalent condition in everyday life. People develop their identities based on their social status or accomplishments, which are fragile and fleeting. I was riding an emotional rollercoaster in the past or the future, but rarely in the present. The more success I had, the higher the expectations I placed on myself. I worked so hard for so many years to become an elite college golfer. In the process I learned the pitfalls associated with the destructive syndrome, "I'll be happy when..." I believed that once I achieved at a high level in golf, I would be happy. I was caught in a vicious cycle. This was the first time in my life I had lost my way. I prayed humbly with an open heart and open mind; God answered.

On a gusty spring afternoon a Kansas sunflower blew into my room at the Sigma Chi House. With blonde hair, a tan and athletic body, and an incredible smile, she was beautiful in every physical sense, but my attraction to her was fueled equally by her positive energy. Jacqueline Brammell was truly amazing. She was the happiest person I had ever encountered; she exuded an infectious positive energy. Everywhere she went the world returned the smile she greeted it with. In a few months I

The coolest girl in the world

was dating my soul mate who would eventually become my wife. Jacqy taught me many things, but one of the most impactful lessons was that a positive attitude does not follow success; rather, it precedes it.

12.

VOLITION

It's choice—not chance—
that determines your destiny.

—JEAN NIDETCH

As I matured, I became more aware of God's messengers. A life-altering moment of synchronicity came in the classroom. A remarkable professor named David Cook was about to teach me a skill that would empower my life forever.

I sat watching the hands of the big black-and-white clock on the wall steadily inching forward with no sign of the professor. A few minutes late, a good-looking young professor breached the doors. He strode calmly and purposefully to the front of the room without acknowledging the ruckus class. He picked up a piece of chalk and wrote the word VOLITION on the board. He then turned toward us and waited calmly for the class to settle down. Then we waited in silence.

"Does anybody know what the word *volition* means?" he said, gesturing toward the black board.

The class returned his volley with a salvo of silence.

"C'mon! It's only the most powerful word in the world!" Dr. Cook was baiting us, clearly in control of the chess match, enjoying the exchange.

"Well, what is it?" the class collectively rumbled.

After panning the room and engaging our souls through several more moments of restless anticipation, he finally enlightened us.

"Volition is the power to choose," he revealed at last. "And every day we have choices. Do not waste this gift. Throughout your life, your choices will define you. Your choices become your life's story. Each day you can:

...choose to be positive or negative,

...choose to love or to hate,

...choose to be constructive or destructive,

...choose to take care of your mind and body or be sedentary,

...choose to build people up or to tear them down,

...choose to have faith."

I remember the sound of the big swinging double-doors brushing against one another as Dr. Cook left the room and the silence that followed after the doors came to a stop. Life's choices offer each of us limitless power to control our destiny. We become our choices and our choices become our legacy. Volition, the power to choose, is the single most powerful portal to your quintessence. The choice is yours.

13.

THE BBQ TOURS

★

*Faith is deliberate confidence in the character of God, whose
ways you may not understand at the time.*

—OSWALD CHAMBERS

I had been a good golfer for many years, but my work habits
starting paying big dividends my last year at Kansas. I qualified for the Centennial United States Amateur Championship
in Newport, Rhode Island, where I played against a kid named
Tiger Woods. He won. I did manage to best Tiger in a round
that year. That fact won't buy me a Coke, but it's still a pretty cool
for a walk-on who started playing golf with four cut-off clubs.

Later that season I shared medalist honors at the Kansas
Invitational. That year I was ranked in the top echelon in the
Rolex Amateur Rankings and made the cut at the NCAA
Championships with my teammates from KU. I had made
the transformation from good golfer into a true competitor.
I give a lot of credit to my brother-in-law Bob Harstad for
teaching me how to compete.

A Patriot's Calling

The youngest of nine children, Bob Harstad grew up in Loveland, Colorado, with his mother Maria and eight siblings. His dad had passed away when he was five. Despite their best efforts, the Harstads struggled with even the most basic needs. Since Bob was 6'6", hand-me-downs weren't available. Bob wore shorts every day, even in the brutal Colorado winters.

Athletics provided Bob with a way out. His success was fueled by desperation rather than inspiration. He clawed his way out of Loveland and attended Creighton University in Omaha Nebraska. He started every game for the Bluejays over his four-year career—128 straight!

Bob was a team player. He went all out, all the time. He dove for every loose ball and fought for every rebound. Dick Vitale called him the Windex Man for his ability to "clean the glass." Bob understood that the object of basketball was to out hustle, out play, and outscore the opponent. He worked his tail off to accomplish those goals every time he took the court.

His bust-your-butt attitude resulted in his admission to an elite club. He became only the fourth player in the 100+ year history of the Missouri Valley Conference to score over 2,000 points and get over 1,000 rebounds. His acceptance speech at the MVC Hall of Fame ceremony in 2007 referred to "that fourth guy." Trivia buffs know that Oscar Robertson, Larry Bird, and Xavier McDaniel have all accomplished that feat. But Bob Harstad? How did the kid from Loveland, Colorado, reach that level? I know how. I saw it first hand and did my best to emulate it. Through hard work, persistence and diligence, Bob Harstad made himself the best he could possibly be. In the end, you can't do more than that.

Professional golf had always been a dream; it was the next step in my evolution. After I had finished my master's degree in sports psychology under the direction of my mentor Dr. David Cook, I hitched a ride on Southwest Airlines to Scottsdale, Arizona, where I was fitted for the precision instruments I would swing in order to make a living. Going through the toy box at the PING golf-club factory was like having Christmas in July. I was all geared up, complete with a beautiful white tour bag with my name on it. I certainly looked like a professional golfer. No excuses. I was equipped to succeed.

Bob taught me how to compete.

In professional golf, the mini-tours are analogous to the minor leagues in baseball. We called them "The Barbeque Tours." There was a running joke on tour that in two years we played every bad course in every bad town in America. The truth is that we played some great courses and visited some great towns. My fellow golfers and I were nomadic characters, traversing the country like a traveling fraternity. Our caravan rolled into town on Wednesday,

73

and we played golf through Sunday. This golf safari went on for about eight months out of the year.

Over the next year and a half I put thousands of miles on my bug-stained white Toyota 4Runner and made some great memories and friends. Having spent so many summers on the great American road as a kid, part of me always felt like I was home when I was touring. As I zigzagged my way across the country on the BBQ tours, I had plenty of time to think. It was during these mile marker-induced trances that the whisper calling me to serve gradually became louder. I believed that I had the ability to make the PGA Tour, but I felt in my heart that God had a different plan. A fire of discontent was burning in my soul, calling me to take action and change my course. I had the courage to listen.

When I failed to make it through the PGA Tour Qualifying School in 1997, I hung up my professional spikes. After almost two years, I finished with $228 in my bank account. I had made a living playing golf. More importantly, I had learned a lot about Dan Rooney. I had pushed myself physically, emotionally, and spiritually. I had lived in the realm between fear and faith.

It wasn't easy to give up the dream of professional golf, but I had listened to Mom and given it my best effort. I had taken purposeful action for almost 21 years and had realized my dream of becoming a competitive golfer. It was time, and I was ready for the next chapter in my life. I have a good friend Dennis who will tell you that if things in life don't go as planned, it's okay. Speaking from experience, he will be the first to say, "Pick yourself up and find a new dream."

Coach Randall, Slade Adams, Kit Grove,
Chris Thompson, Alan Stearns, and me.

14.

DREAMS

★

"Try something that is impossible"

—DENNIS WALTERS

From the time he was eight years old, Dennis Walters was fascinated with golf. In his mind, it was only a matter of time before he would be walking the best courses in competition with the elite in the field. He worked on his game, studied the greats, and made a name for himself as an amateur player. Dennis turned professional shortly after school with dreams of one day tearing up the PGA Tour. His initial qualification attempt brought him to the finals, but he failed to make the cut. Never one to run from a challenge, Dennis was more determined than ever. Knowing he had more work to do, he spent some much needed time on the mini-tours and even went to South Africa to improve his game.

That all changed dramatically when he was just twenty-four years old. After finishing a tournament just several days before his second attempt at PGA Tour Qualifying School, he decided to meet his good friend Ralph Terry at Roxiticus

Golf Club for a few more holes of golf. Dennis is still unclear on exactly what happened that day, but on his way out to meet Ralph, who was putting out on sixteen, something went horribly wrong. The next thing he knew, Dennis woke up on the ground next to an overturned golf cart, unable to get up. A dog heard the commotion, and barked. The forecaddie in Ralph's group, hearing the dog's plea, called for Ralph, who rushed to the scene. A doctor was summoned, evaluated Dennis's condition, and confirmed his worst fears. He was paralyzed from the waist down.

Although he had suffered severe spinal cord damage, Dennis initially remained optimistic. He thought his condition would improve. After several months in the hospital, followed by several more in rehab, Dennis became frustrated and confronted one of his doctors. As Dennis describes it, when the doctor told him that he would never be able to walk again, it made him cry. But when the doctor told him that he was never going to play golf again, it made him mad. Defiant, he told the doctor, "Yes, I am."

It was no secret how great a golfer Dennis was or how much he wanted to play professionally. And nobody knew more than Dennis of the potential and the dreams that were instantly destroyed. He was saddened, depressed, even suicidal. Dennis was facing an incredible test. He would fight physical, emotional, and spiritual battles. His faith would be his shield. With the help of his mom Florence, his dad Bucky, his sister Barbara and the support of his friends, instead of giving up all hope of a fulfilling life, Dennis adopted a new mantra; he would find a new dream. But it would not be easy.

He would intermittently experience despair in the darkest depths of his soul.

In his most trying hours, Dennis received a glimmer of motivation: a letter from Ben Hogan, who after suffering a near fatal accident of his own in 1949, had made a tremendous comeback to golf. The letter, written in August of 1974, read as follows:

Dear Denny,

Just recently I learned of your unfortunate accident and with your permission I would like to offer my thoughts and a word of encouragement.

We know the human body is a great machine and can absorb many shocks. Even though it may seem slow, recovery is possible provided one has faith, hope, will and determination.

From what I have heard about you I am sure you possess these qualities, so please keep battling and you will soon overcome this bad interlude in your life.

All good wishes for your future.

Sincerely,
Ben

Dennis was so touched and uplifted by this extraordinary outreach from his hero that tears literally rolled off his cheek onto the paper and are visible through the glass of the frame that now holds the letter.

He was beginning to come to terms with the fact that he would no longer be able to do certain things, but there was no way he was going to give up playing golf. Lying in bed, dreaming of one day getting back on the golf course, he squeezed the grip of a golf club until his hands hurt. With his own version of a security blanket in hand, he did his best to manage his emotional distress.

One day while watching the Bing Crosby Tournament with his dad, Dennis saw his college buddies playing on TV and he completely broke down. Unable to bear the pain of his son, Bucky convinced Dennis to get outside and test the limits of his wheelchair at the nearby clubhouse. His first few attempts to hit golf balls into a net were futile; he couldn't clear his legs. So his dad went home and brought back a pillow to prop him up. With the extra height, he was at least able to swing the club, but he couldn't keep his balance. So back home Bucky went. This time, he brought back a strap to hold up Dennis. This provided great leverage to swing the club, but he almost tipped over the chair in the process. They found some rope and tied down the chair. This was the anchor that was needed. After getting the hang of it with tireless swings of the club, Dennis began hitting shots that looked, sounded, and felt great. Just six and a half months after being diagnosed as a T-12 paraplegic, he went down to the hospital parking lot. With his doctor looking on in disbelief, Dennis launched a golf ball out of sight.

That winter Dennis went to Florida and met with Alec Ternyei, who incessantly teed up balls for Dennis. He soon got to the point where he could hit the ball about 180 yards with his driver. He then convinced a couple of high school kids to push him out to the first tee. The hole was 310 yards. Dennis's first shot went right down the middle and brought him more than half the distance. His next shot was a five-wood that ended up just off the green. He then one-handed a wedge up onto the green for a "gimmee." He had just enacted the greatest par in the history of the game. Celebrating this remarkable feat back at the clubhouse, Alec came over and proposed a life-changing concept. Dennis was sitting on a bar stool, which prompted the idea to mount a swivel seat on the passenger side of a golf cart. Three prototypes later, they crafted a seat that was so efficient that Dennis still has it to this day and can now routinely hit the ball 240 yards from his Yamaha golf cart.

But Dennis didn't stop with just the ability to hit the ball well. He taught himself to hit sand shots and putt one-handed while balancing on crutches. He even developed his game to the point where he could break eighty on an average course. He practiced, got better, and began giving demos called, "How to play golf sitting down." Inspired by Joe Kirkwood and Paul Hahn Sr., two great trick shot artists, Dennis came up with the idea of performing his own shows to inspire others, kicking off the next phase in his journey. This developed into the Dennis Walters Golf Show, where he performed "shots from unusual lies."

His first show in 1977 was set up by Dr. Gary Wiren at the PGA Merchandise Show at Disney World, where he performed with Bob Toski and Jim Flick. While the show received a great response from the crowd, he faced many obstacles heading into the future; mainly, no one would hire him. That was until his dad wrote a letter to Jack Nicklaus seeking guidance in helping Dennis fulfill his new dream. Not only did Dennis get a reply, but MacGregor Golf Company signed Dennis to a $25,000 contract, increasing his shows up to one hundred per year. His has now performed over 2,700 shows in forty-nine states.

While his dad is now gone, Dennis has adopted the help of a new caddie, his dog, who has become an important part of the show over the years. After braving the trail with his dogs Muffin, Mulligan, and Benji Hogan, Dennis now has found Bucky, named in honor of his father. Dennis rescued Bucky from an animal shelter after an exhaustive search. An animal lover, Dennis spreads the message of the shared joy between humans and animals. He likes to say he can exist without a dog, but he cannot live without one.

Dennis Walters loves the sport of golf and does a wonderful service in promoting the physical, mental, and social aspects of the game. One of the most difficult things to come to terms with for Dennis was realizing that he would never play golf as good from his seat as he did standing up. He finally realized that he was looking at things in the wrong way. The important thing was not how he used to play, but rather how he would play in the future and whether he could improve. Once he understood this, he saw a dramatic improvement and felt much better about things.

The message of his show is simple: "If there is something in your life that you really want to do, no matter how impossible it may seem, if you are willing to work hard, persevere and hang in there, you can achieve success, achieve your dreams, and achieve anything that you want to do. If you stop and think about it, anything is possible."

Dennis believes that many people view a dream as merely something you have at night, gone when you wake up. But to him, a dream is having a positive thought or a goal in your head and in your heart and doing whatever it takes to make it happen. Everyone told him the same thing: what you are trying to do is impossible. He challenges every member of the audience at each of his shows to be bold. "Try something that is impossible. And if you have a dream and it doesn't work out, never stop dreaming. Find a new dream."

Dennis will tell you to find a new dream, just like he did.

PART TWO

A NEW DREAM

15.

RENO

⭐

The history of free men is never written
by chance but by choice; their choice!
—DWIGHT D. EISENHOWER

As a twelve-year-old back in Stillwater, synchronicity would bring me together with an incredible man during the annual summer Sigma Chi golf tournament. Steve "Reno" Cortright was a fighter pilot in the Oklahoma Air National Guard and made quite an impression on me. He was the prototypical fighter pilot: good looking with the prerequisite fighter-jock aura of confidence that bordered on arrogance. If there were modern-day knights, Reno would have had a seat at the round table. I had confided in Reno during my senior year at the University of Kansas regarding the possibility of following his contrails across the sky. Combine that with a couple hundred viewings of the movie *Top Gun*, and I guess you could say I drank the proverbial Kool-Aid.

In my heart I dreamed of flying, but I had to dig deep to elicit the courage required to cross over into the realm between fear and faith in pursuit of quintessence. Flying an F-16 is a dangerous business, and I was guaranteed that I would be going into combat. It was a noble proposition and a very serious commitment. My paternal grandfather had served and was an inspiration.

Shortly after the Japanese attack on Pearl Harbor, Grandpa Rooney was called to active duty as a captain in the U.S. Army Air Corps and was deployed to serve in England. He was stationed at Bury St. Edmonds, north of London, from mid-1942 until the war ended in 1945. While there, he served as one of the top maintenance officers of the busiest B-17 base in England. He returned home as a colonel in October of 1945. Colonel Rooney served as director of the Northern Illinois Air National Guard until retirement after 30 years of service in the military.

I distinctly remember a photograph of "Grampie" in his full military dress. The silver eagle that denoted his colonel rank sparkled even in the weathered black-and-white photo. His storied military career had fascinated me growing up. As happens with many young boys, my imagination ran wild as I dreamed in the context of Hollywood war heroes fighting against the axis of evil. I was intoxicated by the thought of following in his steps. I dreamed of donning the uniform and "slipping the surly bonds." I wanted desperately to be part of this brave and chivalrous fraternity charged with defending our great nation.

When contemplating a life-altering decision, I have always found it useful to fast-forward and then look back. During this particular soul-searching process I asked myself,

Reno

"If I make it to 85, will I look back and regret not having tried to serve my country as an officer and a fighter pilot?" The answer was an unequivocal yes.

Despite my conviction, I had second thoughts. I had a great life in the world of golf. I was fearful of losing all that I had worked so hard to accomplish. I was afraid of becoming a failure if I washed out of pilot training. Fear and its evil companions almost cost me the opportunity to realize my dreams. But I knew that if I cowered at this moment, I would regret it the rest of my life.

In the end I could not ignore the fire of discontent burning in my soul. I exercised my God-given power of volition. I made a choice to chase my dream.

Steve "Reno" Cortright and Tom Pernice ("Jr.")
at the Patriot Cup.

16.

SPEED
⭐

*The only thing that stands between a man and what he wants
from life is merely the will to try it and the faith to
believe that it is possible.*

—RICHARD M. DEVOS

Jacqy and I packed up my old black Jeep and took off
to Euro-NATO Joint Jet Pilot Training (ENJJPT)
at Sheppard Air Force Base in the great metropolis of
Wichita Falls, Texas. Our address, 1707 Speedway, says
it all. For the next couple years I would be tearing across
the sky at speeds I had only dreamed of. I was venturing
into a completely new realm between fear and faith. As I
learned to fly supersonic jets, I also learned that there was
no way to prepare for the physical, emotional, and spiritual
tests that awaited me in the brilliant blue skies over Texas.

At 0600 on the first day of Undergraduate Pilot Training
(UPT), a roomful of fighter-pilot wannabees sat anxiously in
our dress blues. Never in my life had I been in a room with

more tension. There is no way to tell if you have the right stuff to make it through the gauntlet and become a fighter pilot.

"TEN HUT!"

We all snapped to attention as the colonel walked in.

"At ease," he instructed. "Take your seats."

For the next 20 minutes he welcomed us to one of the most demanding and costly training program in the United States military.

"If you work hard enough, have the aptitude, and make it through the next two and a half years of training, you will be part of the most lethal fighting force in the United States arsenal. Fighter pilots are the pointy end of the spear, and you will be tasked with delivering the president's mail, anytime, anywhere in the world. Taxpayers are contributing millions of dollars to ensure that each one of you is trained and ready to defend not only this country but also all those who can't defend themselves. Prepare yourself for the best and the worst days of your life. You can be sure this training will test you to your limits, but never forget one thing: Today you sit in that chair with the opportunity of a lifetime. Young boys dream of being fighter pilots and flying the fastest, most-modern, most-lethal weapons system on the planet. Each of you now has that opportunity. Cherish it."

Drinking from a fire hose is a phrase used in UPT to describe the amount and velocity of information that you are tasked with comprehending as a student pilot, and that phrase pretty much sums it up. This was a huge change for a college golfer from the University of Kansas. It was the most demanding, exhilarating, frustrating, and fun experience of my life. I started the program with approximately 60 hours of time in a tiny Cessna 152 and was flying supersonic in a T-38 eight months later.

UPT is one enormous test. You must be totally committed to the dream of being a fighter pilot or you won't make it through. You are relentlessly scrutinized and evaluated on everything you do. Academics, simulators, and flying are combined with a general level of student harassment. On a typical summer day we would report at 0430 for a single or double turn (one or two flights) that were bookended by painfully honest briefs and debriefs.

We have an unwritten rule in the fighter-pilot world: "Don't interrupt a brief unless there is a family emergency or the building is on fire." This mentality may seem extreme, but it is one of the reasons the fighter-pilot culture works. Honesty and openness are how we got better at flying each day. After each flight you have a duty as the flight lead to discuss any areas that didn't meet the standard. And it's a high standard. The flight members are relied upon to bring attention to areas where they have failed to execute. Just think how much more efficiently the typical business would operate if everyone shared this level of accountability and honesty. Some days the scrutiny could feel personal, but it was just part of the culture. In the end we were in the business of getting better every flight.

Exhausted from a day's flying, we'd form up and head to academics. At the conclusion of a 12-hour duty day, we were physically and mentally spent. I don't know if this makes sense, but the tank was *below* empty. Yet most nights you were forced to summon the energy to study for the next day's sorties. This cycle went on virtually every day until graduation. As you might imagine, we formed some amazing bonds with our fellow classmates. You meld through adversity and work together as a class to survive pilot training. The colonel was right; I experienced the highest highs and the lowest lows of my life. It is never easy to pour your heart and soul into something and fail. But the UPT program is built to push everyone to the edge and then beyond. The reward of quintessence lies on the edges of life. The real beauty of this type of experience is that if you survive and graduate from pilot training, you have the confidence to do virtually anything.

17.

WINGS

★

Life shrinks or expands according to one's courage.

—ANAÏS NIN

We joked that an instructor pilot's job is to let student pilots try to kill them in the air, intervening just before they do. That statement is closer to reality then you think. Being an instructor pilot is a harrowing concept. Seasoned pilots come back to train students who have no military flying experience. They have to let us push the envelope and make mistakes so that we can begin to sense them on our own. That seat-of-the-pants sensation is what ensures your safety as you are learning the basics. I can't say enough about my instructor pilots; I was blessed to have some great ones. They taught me how to fly, eventually helping me develop airmanship, the culmination of skills that keeps you alive in combat.

Called to service in 1957, the T-37 was affectionately known as the 6,000-pound dog whistle. Its nickname, "The Tweet," is very appropriate, as there was no faster way to turn jet fuel into noise. In the cockpit of these old birds, a distinct smell of Jet-A, hydraulic fluid, and a hint of vomit linger as a reminder of the thousands of young aviators who learned to fly in it. She was a formidable challenge for a kid with virtually no flying experience. The Tweet was fast and had a dizzying instrumentation panel. From the moment I stepped on the ramp, I was "behind the jet," a phrase we use when the plane is moving faster than your brain. My first instructor was a young B-52 pilot, Captain Jim Lobash. We called him "Captain Laidback," and he was a Godsend. He was a great teacher and let me try to kill him at least a dozen times. I was even dangerous on the ground.

Learning to fly the T-37 was a big challenge, but I made it.

The heat waves of West Texas shimmered across the tarmac as we stepped to the jet. The Tweet had a terrible air-conditioning system, and the normal practice was to taxi with the canopy up to help dissipate the searing heat. I was rapidly running through my pre-takeoff checks and nervously squeezed out a radio call. "Cider 21 number one for takeoff."

The tower cleared us to takeoff. As I pushed up the throttles and prepared to release the brakes, my instructor commented that he really liked the cabriolet version of the T-37. "Oh *noooo…*" I looked up and realized that I had been about to attempt to take off with the canopy still up. As I reached up to close the canopy I could feel the wrath of God getting ready to strike. Jim, staring at me like Darth Vader behind the black visor and oxygen mask, said, "Don't worry about it—it's easy to be so focused on the small stuff that you miss the big stuff."

Over the next several months, thankfully, I got a lot better. *Aviate, navigate, communicate* is an approach you learn in the T-37. The essence is that you have to prioritize while you are flying or you could kill yourself. Most successful people apply a similar philosophy in life. They understand how to assess a situation and prioritize what is most important. Life, like a fighter jet, moves at a fast pace. In the connected world we are distracted on an almost constant basis. Success depends greatly on the ability to prioritize and focus our attention on what is most important.

After 6 months, we transitioned from the T-37 to the twin-engine supersonic T-38 Talon. The T-38 is fast—a real fighter. It's the primary trainer for the Air Force and NASA shuttle pilots. My instructor, Scott "Spike" Thomas, is a genuine American hero. About six feet tall, with brown hair and razor-sharp features, he was just how you would imagine a fighter pilot to look. An All-American free safety at the Air

A Patriot's Calling

Force Academy, he went on to become a Viper driver. The official name of the F-16 is the Fighting Falcon, but pilots who fly it call it the Viper because it looks like a snake ready to strike.

Spike inspired all the young guns with his combat stories from Desert Storm.

*1 February 17th, 1991. Operation Desert Storm. One month into the operation and operations were going better than anyone had expected. United States airpower was decimating the Iraqi Military. I was #3 of four F-16s, Callsign Benji 51, tasked to fly reconnaissance on the Euphrates River. I had the good fortune and distinct honor of having Eric "Neck" Dodson as my wingman. Neck was my best friend in the squadron and this was our first combat mission together. We were to launch as a four ship, rendezvous with a tanker for aerial refueling, split into two-ships and prowl the Euphrates River. The Iraqis were replacing the blown up concrete bridges spanning the river with pontoon bridges. Our job was to locate and destroy those bridges, disrupting their ability to move personnel and supplies toward the Kuwaiti theater of operations.

The briefing was routine, but detailed, as are all fighter briefings. Our greatest concern that day was the weather. The weather over Iraq during this period was the worst in a decade, and had affected most of our missions to this point. Takeoff was normal, and we pressed out over the Persian Gulf northbound to the tanker rendezvous point. The ceiling gradually sloped lower as we proceeded, eventually forcing us down to

---

* This story excerpted from a newspaper article by Scott Thomas.

98

1000 feet above the water just to stay out of the clouds. Our flight lead climbed us through the weather in close formation toward our gas station in the air. The milkbowl effect set in quickly—no ground, no blue sky, and no visible horizon with which to orient ourselves. My sense of speed and motion was reduced to believing what my instruments displayed.

Once established on the wing of the tanker, waiting my turn to refuel, I experienced the worst case of the leans I had ever encountered. I perceived the tanker (a KC-10, a military version of the DC-10) to be on its side in 90 degrees of bank, turning into me. Of course I knew this was ridiculous—they wouldn't use more than 30 degrees of bank—but my eyes and inner ears told me differently. One eye on the instruments, one on the tanker, I was actually in straight and level flight! It took five minutes to convince my body and brain to match what my eyes saw. Full of gas, we separated from the tanker and split into two flights of two, Benji 51 and Benji 53. Still in the clouds, we pushed north toward the border. Climbing through 28,000 feet, I, in accordance with my responsibilities as flight lead, decided that if we found clear air prior to the border, we would proceed. If we did not break out of the weather, we would abort the mission and try it again another day. There were very few missions worth hanging it out for at this point in the war.

✪

Through 30,000 feet, Poof!—Clear and beautiful on top. We eventually crested the backside of the weather and were met with unrestricted visual access of the target area. On to the Euphrates River—searching, marking, selecting, and bombing targets. We encountered no hostile fire, just some spurious radar warnings here and there. It was strange to be destroying things in the cradle of civilization. After several passes, we were out of bombs and ready to return to base. Mission accomplished! Well, part of it anyway.

Climbing through 32,000', airspeed 320 knots, 100 miles North of the Saudi Arabia/Iraq border, we were planning to level off above the weather and head directly back to base without hitting the airborne tanker for refueling. This is where things went downhill, both figuratively and literally.

You see, as the pilot of a single engine fighter, any strange noise—a pop or bang—gets your attention in a hurry. I still remember it as "the noise". The metallic "thunk" was paralyzing. I can only describe it as similar to the noise of your car's transmission falling out from beneath and hitting the freeway pavement. The sound was distinct and the accompanying deceleration grabbed my attention immediately, driving my eyes to my engine instruments. I immediately turned south, making a straight line for the Saudi border. As I completed the emergency procedure for an engine malfunction from memory, Neck was flying in tactical formation one mile to my right. While I directed him to close in on me, I further assessed the situation. I had hoped to recognize something familiar and apply additional approved and checklist-directed solutions from simulator training. To my surprise, the engine readings were still in the "green" (normal range). The engine was still turning and burning, but it just wouldn't put out thrust.

Over the next ten minutes, I made several critical decisions, but I don't remember thinking about them prior to making them. The decisions and actions stored in the recesses of my brain and reinforced through continuous training just seemed to spill from my brain to my hands.

Cast of Players

BENJI 53—Capt Scott "Spike" Thomas

BENJI 54—Lt Eric "Neck" Dodson

BULLDOG—Airborne Warning and Control System (AWACS)

BENJI 51—Original Flight Lead

Radio Communications Transcript

BENJI 53—"Benji 4, 3."

BENJI 54—"Go ahead."

BENJI 53—"Dude, I've got an engine problem. I'm turning south." "Bulldog Benji 53."

BULLDOG—"Benji 53, Bulldog. Go ahead."

BENJI 53—"Bulldog, Benji 53 has an emergency. I'm currently 100 north of Customs heading south, 32,000."

BENJI 53—"Neck, rejoin. I'm punching off my tanks."

BENJI 54—"Copy."

BENJI 53—"Neck, I want to get to the nearest border, then maybe KKMC." (King Khalid Military City)

BENJI 54—"I've got Hafr Al Batin closer. Just stay on this heading."

Neck closed in to inspect my jet for damage as I jettisoned my external fuel tanks, reducing my weight and drag. I established a glide and started planning. I was thankful for the training that ingrained in my mind "flexibility is the key to Airpower." I needed it on February 17th 1991. The engine was producing some thrust, just not enough to maintain altitude. No sweat. I set a course for Hafr Al Batin, a small piece of concrete in Northern Saudi. I was going to nurse this baby home and deadstick it in. That option was only available for a short time.

As I flew lower and slower, pieces of metal (compressor and turbine blades) and fuel were spitting out of the tailpipe. I had turned into a $20 million glider. No sweat. I changed the plan. I'll coax it across the border and eject in friendly territory. I honestly gave thought about Neck getting to see a real life ejection seat ride. Just briefly.

Throughout this jaunt, Neck took control of the external communication. He coordinated with the AWACS controller without any direction from me. I never had to tell him what I needed. He knew.

BENJI 51—"Benji 3, 1 Victor."

BENJI 54—"Go ahead."

BENJI 51—"Roger ah, you headin' for Hafr Al Batin?"

BENJI 54—"Ah, negative. Right now we are going straight towards the border, the closest border."

BENJI 51—"I've got the nearest divert for you, Hafr Al Batin one-thirty-four, is that what you've got?"

BENJI 53—"Yeah I got it, I'm not gonna make it."

BENJI 54—"Why not?"

BENJI 53—"I won't make it there, I'm ah looking to get across and get out."

BENJI 54—"Is there something wrong still?"

BENJI 53—"This is all I can get man..... Neck, I'm gonna go a little bit—I'm going less than max range. I guess I should go max endurance."

BENJI 54—"What's your FTIT (Engine temperature) and, ah, RPM say?"

BENJI 53—"Okay, my FTIT is 870, RPM is 94. I'm just not gettin' any thrust. Oil pressure's at 40."

BENJI 54—"Okay, lemme come back and look at you again, okay?"

BENJI 53—"Cool."

BENJI 54—"Dude, I'm gonna punch my tanks off so I can stay with you, all right?"

BENJI 53—"Cool."

Neck soon matched my aircraft configuration, punching his tanks off, sending them tumbling earthward...

BENJI 54—"Ah, what's your gas reading?"

BENJI 53—"46."

I know what you're thinking. You thought fighter pilots always spoke in standardized terms, with tactical jargon, and we do—just not always. From day one in the F-16, I learned communication discipline. We strive for Clear, Concise, and Correct (C3) Comm. This situation called for a different level of "correct" comm. We all have friends and colleagues that we relate to and communicate with on a different level. For Neck and me, this was personal. The first rule of flying and talking is: You have to sound cool. If you sound like a dork, you lose credibility instantly. We all wish we sounded like James Earl Jones but for those of us who don't, we do our best. Throughout this stressful situation, we still communicated effectively. We were clear, concise, and even correct. Though not correct by tactical standards, the messages and information we shared were correct to us.

I knew I wasn't alone. Neck had my back. So did a flight of F-15s, Callsign Exxon. They followed behind us, covering our 6 o'clock. The familiar sound of their radar triggering my radar warning receiver was comforting.

BULLDOG—"And Five-three, you have some friendlies north four."

BENJI 54—"You are leakin' tons of fluid and it looks like gas, that's why I am wondering what your gas is."

BENJI 53—"Okay."

BENJI 54—"It's all comin' out right where the hook meets the engine."

BENJI 53—"Copy. Okay Bulldog, how far do I have to go ... to the border?"

BULLDOG—"Border is 60 miles."

BENJI 53—"I might make it Neck."

BENJI 54—"Yeah, you will Homer man, don't worry." (Neck often called me Homer, invoking cartoon character Homer Simpson)

BULLDOG—"And Benji, ah, your friendlies are tally with you."

BENJI 53—"Copy."

BENJI 54—"Is this all the airspeed you can get?"

BENJI 53—"That's it man. I can dump the nose, but I really don't want to. I wanna keep this wind goin' for me."

I continued milking every mile out of my crippled jet. As time went by, she wasn't responding to my nursing. She needed a surgeon—and I wasn't wearing scrubs. It was obvious that I wasn't going to make it to the border. Neck knew it too. We never spoke of it directly, but we both knew. I resigned myself to the fact that I was jumping out of this bird on the wrong side of the line. We still managed to maintain some levity and humor until the end.

> BULLDOG—"Five-three, ah, confirm you're a single-ship?"

> BENJI 53—"Negative. I've got a wingman here."

> BULLDOG—"Rog."

> BENJI 54—"Ya know Spikey, if you need some more lift, you might want to throw your flaps down."

> BULLDOG—"Five-three, border is, ah, 55 miles."

> BENJI 53—"Copy. Think I'll hang out for a little while, Neck."

> BENJI 54—"Okay."

> BENJI 54—"Say distance to border, Bulldog."

> BULLDOG—"Border 54."

Another communication objective we live by is that information passed should be Situational Awareness (SA) building. Unnecessary or incomplete comm tends to be SA dumping, meaning it reduces or degrades one's mental picture of the current environment. Inexperience is also a factor, as well as responding with what the inquiring mind wants to hear. A perfect example is our young AWACS controller. Ultimately, he did a nice job; however, some of his transmissions were less than effective. A request for Search and Rescue (SAR) was clear. The response was incorrect. Neck calmly requested the controller to coordinate for helicopter support to affect my rescue. AWACS confirmed that the choppers were airborne (not true) well before I ejected.

> BENJI 54—"Understand you've got choppers in the air?"

> BULLDOG—"Benji, you want choppers?"

> BENJI 54—"That's affirm. You guys better scramble them now!"

> BULLDOG—"Rog."

> BENJI 54—"Vector 'em to where we're gonna be."

> BENJI 54—How you doin' Homer?"

> BENJI 53—"Hangin' in man."

> BENJI 54—"Cool. I'm with you all the way."

How many co-workers will stay by your side as you're going down in flames? Words can't express the calm and confidence that fell over me when he made that call to me.

> BENJI 53—"I'm gonna try the flaps (interrupted)."

> BULLDOG—"Benji, border 50."

Neck inquired about known threats in our path.

> BENJI 54—"Copy 50. Bulldog, Benji."

> BULLDOG—"Benji, go ahead."

BENJI 54—"Copy, understand that ah, this border area is pretty clear with threats?"

BULLDOG—"That's affirm, I'll check for ya."

BENJI 54—"Check please."

BENJI 53—"Flaps help a little bit Homie."

BENJI 54—"Cool."

BENJI 53—"My AOA (angle of attack) is down a little bit."

BULLDOG—"And Five-three, we're checkin' for ya."

BENJI 53—"Okay."

Our original flight lead, Benji 51, monitored our comm. He stayed out of our business until he needed information, or could provide help.

BENJI 51—"Benji 4, 1."

BENJI 54—"Go."

BENJI 51—"Anything we can do to help?"

BENJI 54—"Say again?"

BENJI 51—"Anything I can do to help?"

BENJI 54—"Ah, you might wanna get on a tanker, get some gas and be able to, ah, help with SAR."

BENJI 51—"Okay."

BULLDOG—"Five-three, border 44."

BENJI 54—"Eight staff, left ten." (threat)

BULLDOG—"Benji Five-three, if you could, squawk emergency please."

BENJI 54—"Do you got that Spike or do you want me to do it?"

BENJI 53—"Yeah, I got it. I dunno if that's such a good idea, is it?"

BENJI 54—"I dunno. Bulldog, Benji, is that a good idea right where we're at?"

BULLDOG—"That's what I was instructed, ah, I'd say no, I've got a good contact with you."

BENJI 54—"Okay, good, keep that contact. Do you got choppers in the air?"

BULLDOG—"Affirm, they are on their way."

BENJI 54—"Copy that."

In the heat of the battle, AWACS asked us to squawk emergency, (code 7700 on the IFF transponder—the same as in civil aviation) which would have highlighted us to every Iraqi watching. Unnecessary. My confidence level in AWACS was sinking. I could tell he was nervous and it seemed like someone was looking over his shoulder, providing poor input to his decision tree. We call it pushing the rope. It's impossible.

Lower and slower I went, trying to stay out of the clouds and remaining aloft as long as I could. Every minute airborne meant a minute less on the ground. I was buying time for the

Search and Rescue (SAR) forces to push north. Neck and I kept track of our distance to the border, and I had a good gouge on my location, which was a plus. However, all of my efforts eventually gave way to the inevitable—this jet was going back to the taxpayers.

For a while, it got too quiet, so I had to break the silence.

BENJI 53—"Bummer dude."

BENJI 54—"What's goin' on man?"

BENJI 53—"Just bummer."

I prepared the cockpit by clearing out everything strapped to my legs and near the seat. Water bottles got stuffed in my pockets, helmet bag, maps and checklists set aside. I tightened my harness straps and cinched down my helmet, ready to take the ride of a lifetime. I was ready. I had no choice.

BENJI 54—"Okay, now you've got fire comin' out of your engine. Looks like it's falling."

BENJI 53—"What's falling?"

BENJI 54—"Well, it looks like you've got sparks and s*** comin' out of your engine now."

BENJI 53—"Okay... Bulldog..."

BULLDOG—"Go ahead."

BENJI 53—"Okay, I'm having a more serious problem now, okay?"

BULLDOG—"Rog."

Tick, tick, tick. Time passed slowly.

> BENJI 54—"Understand, choppers are in the air?"

> BULLDOG—"That's affirm. Border 40."

> BENJI 53—"Neck, you tell me if you see any fire."

> BENJI 54—"Okay, it's red sparks poppin' out right now."

> BENJI 53—"Okay, just tell me if you see a fire."

> BENJI 54—"Okay. Stay with it dude."

My jet shuddered and smoke began to enter the cockpit. The training took over.

> BENJI 54—Okay, you're-"

> BENJI 53—"I-I'm gettin' out!"

> BENJI 54—"Okay, you're on fire."

I instinctively moved my feet to the rudder pedals, back of my head to the headrest, elbows in, reached for the handle and pulled. BOOM!

> BENJI 54—"Okay, Bulldog, we've got him out, we've got him out! He's out of the jet"

"Bulldog, we have a good chute. Bulldog, Benji, do you copy?"

> BULLDOG—"I copy, marked."

I know I closed my eyes. All I saw was red as the ejection seat rocket motor exploded to life. Other pilots who have taken an ACES II ejection seat ride have experienced time compression and felt the seat riding up the rails into the wind. Not me. I felt no time between the initial blast and flying through the air on my back. The free stream wind caught the lip of my helmet, threatening to rip it off. My oxygen mask compressed to my face like a Bo Jackson stiffarm. Luckily, I was only doing 150 knots. Neck saw the show from his "wingside" seat. He said I looked like a rag doll, arms flailing and all. I say I was just waving.

Still breathing. That's good. Checklist! Canopy! Visor! Mask! Seat Kit! LPU! 4 Line Release!

Automatic.

Whoa! What a sight! From between my legs flies a flaming unmanned convertible Viper. It's nothing like in the movies—no soundtrack playing in the background. In fact it's eerily silent. No wind noise because I'm moving the same speed and at the mercy of the wind. The jet vanished into the clouds trailing flames the length of the jet. I looked down and saw so much detail. The ejection seat, trailing its drogue chute was plummeting to the ground. Behind it, the canopy tumbled out of control. I hope no one is on the ground to greet the uninvited American.

The ride from 12,000 feet seemed to take an eternity. Snow was falling and swirling in the clouds. My harness was digging into my crotch. I cautiously moved the straps around to make more of a seat. I felt like I might fall out of the straps while adjusting them; an irrational thought, I know, but the brain works in strange ways. I emerged from the clouds at around 3000 feet above the ground. The surface resembled the moon—very rocky and surprisingly hilly. I struggled to maneuver the parachute with the steering cords, finding that I could only turn right. I figured it would behoove me to be good at right turns, so I practiced them. Scouting the area, I noticed a grouping of black spots in the dirt. Old campfires? Hopefully very old.

Approaching the ground, I again reverted to my ingrained life support and parachute training. Eyes on the horizon. Eyes on the horizon. Of course, my curiosity got the best of me. The rocks below looked pretty big. This landing is going to leave a mark. I looked away. Big rocks, big rocks. Looking down again, big rocks. No, small rocks! Eyes on the horizon. Oh great, survive this to break a leg. Knees together, 3-point roll. I hit the ground! A totally uneventful landing. I'll take it.

★

As I sat up in the dusty rocks, my mouth was a dry as the scorched earth surrounding me. Checking myself for injury, I noticed blood on my neck and chest. I only then noticed the gash under my chin—most likely caused by my harness or chinstrap during the ejection sequence. It was the least of my worries at this point. I attempted to gather my chute, but the risers had become intertwined in the rocks. I decided to conserve energy, assess my surroundings, and drink some water. I performed our established communication procedures, and radioed to Neck that I was okay on UHF 243.0, the emergency frequency. Needing a more discrete frequency,

I audibled Neck to our secondary emergency frequency: UHF 282.8.

Silence. We crave it sometimes. In my world it was so silent it was loud. I heard tones and ringing in my ears. I was in a lonely place—for a while, anyway. Out of the clouds comes Neck, hauling ass below the weather to help me out. He scouted the area, exposing himself to the threat of anti aircraft artillery and surface to air missiles. He didn't have to do it.

He just did.

I was surrounded by excellence.

He accurately marked my position using latitude and longitude from the inertial navigation system.

We determined it would be best for me to stay put. The immediate area was clear for the time being. No need to beat feet for safer surroundings. I eventually gathered my parachute and inventoried my supplies. I had a full survival kit with plenty of water, a smaller kit known as a Hit and Run kit, which contained only essentials, and my survival vest. The vest held a 9mm pistol with extra clips, signaling devices (flares, mirror, and a strobe), the survival radio, and a compass. Assessing the threat, my highest threat wasn't the enemy; it was what we call environmentals. The weather we overflew to enter Iraq was moving my way. I had to remain dry. Hypothermia... I sure didn't consider the possibility when I took off and the temperature was 85 degrees. I was positioned in a depression where someone would have to be within 500 yards to see me. I had nowhere to go though, nowhere to hide... Except—in the middle of the desert I had a seemingly useless item that was potentially lifesaving. We often flew over the Persian Gulf, and were equipped with one-man life rafts integral to our survival kit. I flipped the raft over, and propped it against a tumbleweed. It served as a great lean-to. The spray shields hung down, acting as a sort of curtain. I was able to get all of my gear inside, minus a portion of the parachute. I became a black dot in a sea of wasteland—The proverbial needle in a haystack.

Assuming the choppers were on the way, I prepared for my pickup. What do I need? Take the Hit and Run kit, and my helmet, so I can fly again. That should do. On the horizon to the west, I watched the thunderstorm brewing. I knew I was close to Kuwait and a north/south running road was a few miles west of me. Anticipating a quick pickup, I stuffed a handful of rocks into my G-suit pocket. I had to get souvenirs after going through all this.

Under my raft, I leaned back against my survival kits, propped my helmet under my knees, and waited in my combat recliner. I used this time to check out my survival vest. This was the first time I seriously thought about confronting the enemy and being captured. Most of the decisions I made up to this point were easy because they were solutions prescribed repetition and training. The subsequent choices were on me. I ensured my 9mm pistol was loaded and considered my options if confronted. The last thing I wanted was to be on a flatbed truck getting hauled away by the enemy. If two show up, I'll fight—kill them then trek south. If three or more show up armed, I'll do whatever it takes to stay alive. Was that weak? Should I fight? On my soil, Yes. On theirs, No. Many of my brothers in arms had already shown up on CNN, beaten, but alive. I would take my chances. I wouldn't let them defeat my will.

Here comes the rain—big drops. I love a great thunderstorm, just not this one. I struggled to hold the raft down. As the cold gusts of wind tried to pry it away, lightning struck nearby and I felt the hair on my arms rise up from the static electricity. I slowly put my radio aside. I was holding the only metal lightning rod within miles. I was laughing inside for a moment. The storm was as strong as it was quick. I achieved victory! I was completely dry. The skies cleared as night fell, revealing more stars than I knew existed—a hauntingly beautiful sight.

I strictly followed the emergency radio procedures. Listen at preset times, otherwise sit tight and wait. The Iraqis had the ability to home in on radio transmissions and locate the source. I hadn't transmitted since talking to Neck, who had handed me off to another flight for cover. I was glad it was dark. Due to the risk and recent problems with resistance during daylight rescue attempts, no one was coming until darkness fell. I was comforted by the faint sound of jet noise—the sound of freedom—high above me.

I was surrounded by excellence.

One hour gone. I expected a ride by now. Are they coming? The storm must have delayed them. I hope it slowed up everyone else too. They can't find me. Silence. Prayer. My wife. My baby daughter. My wedding ring. I always wear it. We are supposed to take them off, for safety reasons mostly. An even more important factor was security in the case of capture. The enemy would play on your fears and fabricate lies about the safety of your family if they knew you were married. I took off my ring and stored it in my pocket. At the first sign of trouble, I would swallow it. I'd do whatever it took to retrieve it as nature took its course. It was that important to me.

More waiting. Nothing over the radio. Silence—and a lesson in responsibility. In the darkness, I dropped my compass. I also misplaced my strobe light. Nice job Spike. I dropped these critical objects, but never lost them. Each item contained in my survival vest was attached to its respective pocket by a thin lanyard. I simply pulled the lanyard and presto!—there was my gear. Simplicity at its finest. Someone, most likely an airman who earned $12,000 a year, was responsible for tying off our survival gear with simple knots and string. That single person took his responsibility seriously. His or her devotion to duty, no matter how mundane or tedious, was crucial to my survival.

I was surrounded by excellence. "Excellence in all we do".... It matters.

Time passed slowly. My day had started early. I was comfortable and tired. I did the "jerk"—that spasm you sometimes experience when you fall asleep. Not good. I stuck my head out of the raft for some cool air. Waiting for my ride home was a lot like waiting for someone to pick you up and drive you somewhere. Clock watching, confusion, impatience. Then when your ride shows, the past disappears and you get in and go, focusing on the task at hand. My ride was the same. It was a sound I had heard before—on the TV show MASH.

The helicopters were unmistakable, the rotor blades cutting through the dusty night air south of my position.

It was like music. I grabbed my Hit and Run kit, helmet and radio. The Blackhawks (helicopters) were maybe 200 yards away heading northeast.

"Benji 53 is up! I'm on your left! Turn left!"

Why aren't' they talking to me?

"You passed me up! You passed me!"

They disappeared.

The strobe!

I activated my strobe.

"My strobe is on! Come back left!"

I never heard a response. What a great radio—if I needed a doorstop. Silence...

Then the music reappeared. Like the rising sun over a knoll, a helicopter filled the sky. The tips of the rotor blades were lit up like a ring of fire as the sand billowed upward. The first Blackhawk flew directly over me, too close to turn and land. I had moved away from my raft so as not to get hit by it if it blew around.

"I'm holding the strobe! I'm holding the strobe!

✪

Crouching on one knee, I saw the second chopper appear. Following some world class maneuvering, it set down 20 yards away. I shielded myself from the pelting sand, still holding the strobe. No one came to get me for what seemed like several minutes. I was trained to stay put until the pararescue crew approached me, but that green light pointing my way from the cockpit was too inviting. They must not want to get out. As I emerged from my crouching position, a figure appeared from opposite the chopper and grabbed me by the arms. This man with arms the size of my legs spun me around to face him. I knew the Cyclops-like figure was friendly. His single eye was a night vision device. The first word out of his mouth was "Sir".

I was surrounded by excellence.

"Sir, are you okay?"

"Yes, I'm Benji 53, let's get the hell out of here!"

With his guidance, I ran to the chopper. Break for daylight! I've been here before...

The soldier directed me to sit on the floor where I was flanked by my escort and another "Snake Eater" (Army Special Forces) who jumped in via the left hand door. He had sprinted to my raft first. When he came up empty, the second soldier emerged to circle around and recover me. After jumping back in, he couldn't get the door closed. Just go. The Medic immediately tended to me, offering water and food, examining my injury, and making me comfortable. Two

Mini-Gunners were positioned mid-cabin, left and right with two pilots at the controls. Seven warriors in each Blackhawk. Fourteen men sent to rescue one. I'm still humbled.

As we lifted off, I was unaware of any threat in the immediate area. I cheered my rescuers, thanking them, and celebrating, when the professional next to me simply reached over and placed his hand on my chest. Without a word, I knew what he meant. Spike, sit down, shut up and color. I quickly realized that even though I felt finished, they weren't. We departed southwest bound in a hurry. From the north, a SAM launch! Flares dispensing, the pilot maneuvered defensively, watching the missile hit the desert floor. The angels who lifted me from earth sped south a mere 20 feet off the ground at 180 knots in complete darkness. The cold breeze from the open door made me feel more alive than I had ever felt in my life.

I was surrounded by excellence.

Spike was one of the lucky few pilots picked up by pararescue.

No one on that helicopter so much as blinked until we reached the border. As we climbed up to altitude, I knew we were home free. I finally got to thank the crew as we proceeded to King Khalid Military City in northern Saudi. I had flown missions out of KKMC just ten days earlier, and knew that some squadron pilots would be there. To my surprise, my wingman, Neck emerged from the crowd to meet me. I could have kissed him. Neck had diverted to KKMC after burning every last drop of his available fuel overhead my position in Iraq. There couldn't have been a better reunion.

It turns out that Neck was able to listen to the entire rescue at the Special Forces Command Post. The Special Forces had teamed up with an Army Aviation Unit from Savannah, Georgia, and trained for the SAR. The whole world anticipated huge U.S. aircraft losses to Iraqi air defenses. Based on those estimates, we, as a military, feared we wouldn't have the number of SAR crews required. So through their commitment and some raw chance, the boys from Fort Campbell, Kentucky received the orders to go find me that night.

★

Through debriefing at the Special Forces command center, I discovered information previously unknown to me. Two separate groups were hunting me, one from the south, and the other from the north. The rescue crew estimated I had an hour before they ran across me. Upon receiving the "all clear" from the SAR forces, my brothers above—the invisible jet noise, rolled in and eliminated the unlucky soldiers looking to track me down. The helicopters hadn't launched as was reported by AWACS. In fact, after landing at KKMC, Neck saw the rescue helicopters on the ground. They had been delayed by the weather and an aircraft malfunction requiring maintenance prior to launching. The crew in the Blackhawk was calling me on their way in to the rescue zone. Neither of us heard the other. Following the debriefing, I was fed some fine United States Army cuisine, stitched up and released to the Air Force side of the base. I was able to call my wife. She initially thought I was joking around. I was glad I was the one passing the news to her. It was a good thing I kept my helmet. I got to fly combat missions again one week later.

After every mission we fly, we debrief the flight to come up with Lessons Learned. Lessons Learned are statements regarding mission execution that can be shared with the entire squadron or used individually. They reveal our errors and provide solutions to correct those errors, or simply reinforce the techniques and procedures that make us successful. They are pieces of the unsolved jigsaw puzzle. Each piece provides us with a clearer picture and pushes us toward excellence in our mission execution. Communication and decision making. These two core principles inherent in our operations were vital to my successful ejection and subsequent rescue.

My lessons learned during my time with Spike
are with me everyday

The day I graduated from pilot training I realized the dream of becoming a military aviator. On May 5, 2001, Spike gave me a set of aviator wings and a small piece of paper with his parting advice.

SPIKE'S GUIDE

→ SHUT UP & LISTEN

→ DO NOT TRY TO BE LIKE SOMEONE ELSE. FIGURE OUT WHO YOU DO NOT WANT TO BE LIKE, THEN BE YOURSELF AND AVOID THEIR PITFALLS.

→ NEVER RUN OUT OF GAS, OR ALLOW YOUR FLIGHT LEAD TO RUN YOU OUT OF GAS.

→ CALL YOUR PARENTS EVERY WEEK.

My entire family came down to Wichita Falls for graduation weekend. The base hosted a "Red-Carpet Day" the day before graduation. The squadron recreates a typical day at UPT—minus the harassment—and family and friends are invited for a day in the life of a student. Visitors get to fly the simulators, try on the flying gear, and go out on the flight line to watch the jets fly.

My family was luckier than most because Scott "Rookie" Rooks and Bruce "Boston" Butters came down for my graduation. They flew down the F-16D model (two-seater) from the Oklahoma Air Guard. Fritzie, 87 at the time, had been in a wheelchair all day. When the group headed out to tour the jet, he jumped out of his chair like a 12-year-old running out of class on the last day of school. He fired up that ladder to get a glimpse inside the cockpit. The F-16 has a way of keeping you young.

Boston and Rookie at UPT Graduation

To celebrate my pending wings, Rookie took me on an F-16 ride, and my family got to watch as we "slipped the surly bonds" and went straight vertical on takeoff. On graduation night, Rookie and Boston pinned on my wings. We had a huge night playing CRUD, a full-contact pool game played around a modified snooker table, one of many great traditions in the world of fighter pilots. This raucous fast-paced game originated in the Royal Canadian Air Force. A typical night includes a few minor injuries with the occasional blown-out knee…but we never spill a single drop of our beverages. The entire family celebrated into the night. It was another great stride in the pursuit of quintessence.

UPT Graduation with Dad, Mom, Kate, Bob, Beth, and Jacqy.

18.

FIGHTER COUNTRY U.S.A.

★

*All the strength and force of man
comes from his faith in things unseen.*

—JAMES FREEMAN CLARKE

The vibrant blue skies of Arizona serve as a vast school-house for our nation's future fighter pilots. The sound of jet noise, or as fighter pilots call it, the sound of freedom, echoes off the scorched dessert mountains. Luke Air Force Base is the world's largest fighter training base. More than 185 F-16s line its ramps and make Luke one inspiring site.

I remember pulling onto base and gazing up from my vintage Porsche 911 Cabriolet. I coasted to the shoulder of Falcon Drive, and my eyes were transfixed on the distant horizon as two Vipers came in for landing. Those steel birds were in perfect fingertip formation. Fingertip requires pilots to fly with just three feet of wingtip clearance. This is but one example of the trust that permeates the fighter-pilot nation and a powerful demonstration of the maxim, *"You have to trust people in your life to succeed."*

When I saw the Vipers in formation, I could not help but smile because I knew I would soon be flying that awe-inspiring jet. I had been chasing a dream, and I was about to catch it. I was also smiling for another reason: on our way out west, Jacqy and I learned that she was pregnant. We were expecting in April.

I was assigned to the 63d Fighter Squadron. As a member of the Panthers, I had little time to catch my breath. The fire hose was turned on yet again. More information was coming at me than my brain could process. We started with a month of academics, learning every system of the F-16. I was frustrated; I didn't want to *build* it, I wanted to *fly* it. But this was all a part of required hazing, the initiation into the elite fighter-pilot society.

Before we knew it, it was time to hit the flight line. After just four flights with an instructor in the D model (two-seat version) I was cleared to go solo. It was hard to believe that after a whopping seven hours in the Viper they were going to let me take up a $40 million fighter—by myself! Of course my instructor would be in the chase plane, but in the end it would be up to me to ensure that my number of takeoffs were paired with an equal number of landings.

November 17, 2001, is one of the days I found quintessence. It was the culmination of pushing myself to the limit physically, emotionally, and spiritually. Never had I worked so hard for something and wanted something so much.

As I stepped out on the tarmac that day, I took a deep breath. I was met with a heavy dose of JP-8 jet fuel that penetrated my olfactory senses...*ahhhh*...the unmistakable smell of speed. The familiar hiss of Vipers ripped across the sky in the distance as I anxiously approached my assigned fighter. With its sheer and precision construction, the Lockheed Martin-designed F-16 Fighting Falcon is aesthetically unrivaled. Its silhouette commands fear, respect, mystery, and excitement all at once. I have confessed to my Jacqy and my priest, Father Jack, that the F-16 is the sexiest thing I have ever seen. It is a majestic combination of form and function.

After a thorough walk around to pre-flight the F-16, I climbed the ladder, nestled into the cockpit, strapped on the jet, and completed my pre-flight checks. It was time to fly. Solo.

We slowly taxied out to the runway and were positioned for takeoff. The butterflies intensified in my stomach as the anticipation grew. The F-16 has 29,000 pounds of thrust, and in a clean configuration without external fuel tanks it weighs about 28,000 pounds. It has a greater than one-to-one thrust-to-weight ratio. This allows the F-16 to accelerate while going straight vertical. I was a man on a rocket.

I rechecked that my straps were secure and that the ejection seat was armed. I pushed the throttle up to 80 percent and checked the engine one last time...*looks good*. Next, I slowly moved the throttle to military power...*good oil-pressure rise*. Then I lifted the throttle up and over the detent to initiate maximum thrust lighting the afterburner, and I immediately felt the fire-breathing beast come to life.

I started rolling, quickly picking up speed as the multiple stages of afterburner kicked in, each slamming me further and further back against the seat. I gave the obligatory *"YEE-HA!"* while hurtling down the runway. In the span of just 1,600 feet I passed through 150 knots (172.5 miles per hour), and as I gently pulled back on the stick, this perfect flying machine soared into the sky. I sucked up the landing gear, and my dreams took flight. I was careening toward the wild blue yonder on my first solo Viper ride.

The F-16 is a veritable magic carpet—a miracle machine capable of sustaining nine Gs. It was the first jet to exceed the physiological capabilities of the pilot. After a 9-G sortie, your body is covered with "geasles." The extreme g-forces break thousands of capillaries, which leaves tiny red spots all over your skin. They are harmless, a simple reminder of fun you had turning and burning. The F-16 has a top speed of 1,400 miles per hour (Mach 2.1), over twice the speed of sound.

As I climbed into the sky, the altimeter was spinning like pennies on a gas pump. The F-16 can climb to 50,000 feet in less than one minute. Defying gravity together, we obliterated the theories of Sir Isaac Newton. I had never felt more alive in my life.

Magic carpet.

It was a religious experience, an ascension into the heavens. I was engulfed by a perfect bubble canopy that offered me an omnipotent view of the world. Sitting on the tip of a spear, flying on the razor-sharp edge of instability, my thoughts became motion. The F-16 pulled me into a vortex separated from the rest of the world. I could feel the Viper, like a drug, seeping into my veins. One taste of this sacred world and I was addicted. When I touched down an hour later, it was like time had stood still. Afterward, I yearned to get back in that time machine, to that place only fighter pilots understand.

As I climbed down from my magic carpet, I remembered the colonel's talk a year and a half earlier. I thought, "I'm living every boy's dream." I still had another eight months of training at Luke, but I knew in my heart that that year two dreams would come true: I would become an F-16 fighter pilot, and soon after, I would become a dad.

My airmanship continued to grow at about the same pace as Jacqy's belly. We enjoyed our weekends. Friday afternoons we would load up the Jeep and chase the sunset to San Diego. For a couple of people who had spent their entire lives land-locked in the Midwest, nothing felt better than pulling onto the Naval Air Station on Coronado Island. We would watch the sun sink into the Pacific and then head downtown to the Kansas City BBQ. This wasn't just any BBQ joint. It's the one used in filming the piano scene in *Top Gun*. I had come a long way since watching that movie in the Sigma Chi House at KU.

Just after I finished my final F-16 ride as a student, I embarked on another mission. Jacqy and I were scheduled to go into the hospital at midnight on April 5, 2002. We went out and ate our last meal without kids.

Ben Wheatly, a good family friend, gave me some sage advice. "When your baby is delivered, the doctor immediately suctions the amniotic fluid from her nose and throat, so if you are in the right position, you can see your baby take her first breath." My daughter arrived at 12:32 P.M., and I was able to witness her first breath. I had no idea of my capacity to love until she came into my life.

19.

NOONAN

Courage is the first of human qualities
because it is the quality which guarantees the others.

—ARISTOTLE

Following the completion of my training at Luke, I was anxious to get back to my squadron in Oklahoma. I loaded Jacqy and baby Victoria on a plane and hopped into my Jeep, embarking on a great American road trip. With the windows down and a 44-ounce Diet Coke in hand, I pointed east to the heartland with my two black-and-rust Dobermans, Bogey and Sosa. I felt a great sense of accomplishment as I watched Luke disappear in my rearview mirror. Dad always reminded me to celebrate life's moments.

With their ears pinned back and a 70-mile-an-hour breeze blow-drying their wet noses, Bogey and Sosa were in dog euphoria. About five hours outside of Phoenix on I-40 I was singing along with Don Henley when my 95-pound Doberman interrupted the final chorus of *Boys of Summer*. He started panting, whimpering, and pawing my arm. As I pulled off onto the shoulder of the interstate, Bogey dismounted, Dukes of Hazzard style, and scampered off into the weeds, letting go with explosive diarrhea. No big deal; we got that taken care of. Not quite. This exercise repeated itself about every two hours for the next 20+ hours. With regular bathroom stops, intermixed with frequent attempts to keep Bogey hydrated, the trip home was certainly an adventure. There wasn't enough fresh air in the southwestern United States to dilute the aroma. Bogey didn't seem to mind, but it was purgatory for Sosa and me.

Shortly after arriving at the 125th Fighter Squadron in Tulsa, I received my mission qualification training (MQT). MQT is the final stage of training and delves into specifics of how 125th Fighter Squadron fights wars. I was home only a couple months before I shipped out for my first tour in Iraq.

A great philosopher once said, "The height of one's ignorance is not realizing one's ignorance." In the fighter community we call it "all thrust and no vector." Any way you look at it, I was dangerously inexperienced but absolutely full of confidence.

During Operation Northern Watch, we were tasked with patrolling the lawless no-fly zone over northern Iraq. We flew out of Incirlik Air Base, Turkey, known affectionately as "The Lick."

No amount of training can prepare you for it; you just have to go and do it. I remember lying in my bed, staring at the ceiling the night before my first combat mission. My breathing was the only sound; my thoughts my only companion. It was the loneliest and most fearful night of my life. I was not scared of dying. I was terrified of screwing up. The next morning I was "Padre 22" and would be flying my first combat mission on the wing of the mission commander. We would be leading the entire coalition into Iraq. It was the most awesome display I had ever witnessed in my life—the rolling thunder of American airpower comprised of KC-135's, F-16's, F-15's, EA6B's, AWACS, and British Jaguars. We were the pointy end of the spear!

That day one of our mission taskings was to support a reconnaissance flight of British Jaguars, supersonic jets configured with cameras to gather intelligence on the Iraqi forces. They didn't carry any armament, so it was up to us to protect them in case any Iraqi MiGs attempted to engage them as they went in to gather intelligence photos. The Iraqi pilots were combat veterans of the Iraq-Iran War and under the right circumstances could pose a very real threat. They loved to play cat and mouse games bumping up against the no-fly zone. We were thoroughly briefed on their capabilities and ready if they were willing.

My nervous feeling of pending vomit had finally subsided as we intercepted the Brits pushing past Mach 1 and heading into Iraq. A few minutes into the reconnaissance route I began to notice beautiful little white puffy clouds. *That's odd*, I thought. I distinctly remembered the very proper British weather officer's comments from the morning brief: "It will be severe clear day, excellent war-fighting weather for you chaps." Then it hit me. *Holy crap! Those aren't cumulous clouds. They're shooting at us!* At that moment, as bizarre as it sounds, I thought of my sister Kate. I remembered a spring morning that the little twit had called me out the front door moments after intentionally stirring up a hornets' nest in a big holly bush. In that same manner the Jaguars were pissing off the Iraqis just in time for us to trundle along and soak up all the antiaircraft fire. It's a surreal moment when you realize someone is trying to kill you.

During my deployment, in addition to enduring the rite of passage of getting shot at, I also received my call sign. The naming ceremony is a rich fighter-pilot tradition. In the same spirit that young Apache warriors would receive new names after their first combat, I would receive mine. Much of the naming ceremony is TOP SECRET, but I will share that you have no say in the process and are at the mercy of the veteran pilots. Your call sign typically combines your personal traits and a "play" on your name. In my case I was the only active fighter pilot/golf professional in the world. My call-sign, "Noonan," comes from the main character, Danny Noonan, in *Caddyshack*, one of the movies that influenced my life.

I made it through my first deployment by the grace of God. I listened and learned and became a better pilot and a better person in the process. Once again I was incredibly blessed to have several experienced pilots mentor me. One in particular was Major Scott "Otter" Stratton.

One of the primary reasons that the fighter-pilot community is so successful is that we genuinely care about each other. We take the time to teach and guide the younger pilots. Scott "Otter" Stratton took me under his wing and on his wing into combat.

Otter is an exceptional fighter pilot. He is indeed a true patriot and without a doubt one of the most capable leaders I have ever followed. He could run a small country if he wasn't busy serving ours. He embraces the world with compassion, kindness, accountability, and faith. He gives praise in public and counsel in private. He leads by example, which I believe is the only true form of leadership. While he has certainly taught me a great deal in the jet, his greatest impact has been outside the cockpit. Otter taught me the power of a positive attitude. He cares about people, and he not only finds something positive in everyone, he also tells them about it. He has a gift of making people feel good about themselves. This may seem simple, but we all know that our lives are often filled with negative reinforcement. Complimenting the qualities you admire in others is extremely powerful.

Scott is one of countless warriors who make the Oklahoma Air National Guard an amazing team. One of the incredible attributes of the Air Guard is that you can serve as a traditional guardsman. You fly eight to ten sorties per month for the guard and have the opportunity to pursue other dreams. While our training requirements are the same as our active-duty counterparts, we are allowed to be in effect part-time, although a part-time fighter pilot is a bit of a misnomer. Flying the F-16 is one of the most demanding and unforgiving jobs in the world. A bad day at the office can leave you as a smoking hole in the ground.

Getting ready to fly a mission with Scott "Otter" Stratton

20.

A PICASSO IN THE ATTIC

★

Choose a job you love, and you will
never have to work a day in your life.

—CONFUCIUS

Dad has always been a source of tremendous insight in my life. One of his most influential maxims can be found in one of his simple, sturdy refrains: "Figure out what you're passionate about and figure out how to do it every day."

My dream was to blend my passions for golf and flying. I wanted to be an F-16 pilot, a PGA professional, and a golf course owner. It was my mission. Thanks to a lot of help from people along the way and hard work my dream worked out.

Dad and I began putting together a group of investors to purchase the Grand Haven Golf Club in Michigan. This was no simple task. It was a big risk. But that didn't deter us. We set a goal. We were passionate. We envisioned our success long before it was a reality.

The next part of the challenge was taking this historic club and revitalizing it. The first time I saw the course, I commented to Dad that it was like finding a Picasso in your grandfather's attic. This particular canvas was beautifully situated in the tree-lined sand dunes along the Lake Michigan shoreline, but years of neglect had taken its toll. My dad is a huge Notre Dame fan and described our vision quest as "waking up the echoes." Our mission would take many years, and we would need a great wingman to act as the mission commander. Dad, Mom, and I scoured the area for a special person to join our mission. Fortunately, our long search brought Chip Ferlaak, a young spirit warrior, into our lives.

Grandpa Rooney had taught Dad some great lessons in interpersonal relationships that he passed on to me. "People don't work *for* you, they work *with* you. Don't be prejudiced in any way. All people and all work have great value. Every working person in society is making a significant contribution to the well-being of all of us."

He couldn't have been more right. Chip proved to be an exceptional recruit for the golf club. But Chip also brought much more into our lives. He and his family have become part of our family. We were looking for a PGA professional. What we got was a life-altering perspective in the maxim of forgiveness.

21.

FORGIVENESS

★

Do not judge, and you will not be judged.
Do not condemn, and you will not be condemned.
Forgive, and you will be forgiven.

—LUKE 6:37

The day was warm and filled with promise. After their regular visit to church, Chip Ferlaak, his wife Jody and their children—Teagan (four), Brock (two), and Wyndham (six months)—ventured out from their hometown of Gaylord, Michigan, for Sunday brunch. A landmark building in nearby Johannesburg, the Old Depot, stood beyond their ordinary path but was an ideal spot to simply enjoy Sunday brunch and experience some great family time.

The restaurant was packed. The Ferlaaks were seated right up front. Amidst a crowd of happy faces and friendly chatter, the children welcomed the parade of entrees that fanned across the table, seemingly covering every square inch of the surface before them. With wide-eyed excitement they went to work on their chocolate-chip pancakes, happily joining the chorus of satisfied friends and families enjoying their meals. This comfortable melody of laughter, dialogue, utensils, plates, and cups suddenly erupted into a terrifying explosion of cracking timber, shattering glass, and twisting metal. Their world exploded around them.

Chip lay unconscious on the hood of a car that was idling in a tangled mess inside the restaurant. Jody, having suffered extensive trauma, opened her eyes to find Teagan contorted on the ground where seconds before her chair had supported her spirit-filled four-year-old frame. Despite her injuries, Jody somehow managed to reach her daughter, but there was nothing she could do. Embracing Teagan's lifeless body, Jody instantly knew that Teagan had already left for heaven. Wyndham, pinned between the grill of the car and the wall, suffered injuries that would leave her with permanent brain damage.

En route to meet with her husband, Cynthia Kundrat had decided to commit suicide by driving her car straight into the restaurant where the Ferlaaks and many others happened to be eating that day. Kundrat survived her attempt to end her own life, but her horrific choice that day brought death to little Teagan and Margaret "Peggy" Koronka, age 29, wife and mother of two. Over the coming months, Chip's, Jody's, and Wyndham's physical injuries would heal, but the psychological impact will surely be felt for generations.

The Ferlaaks endured unspeakable suffering. Jody, who had been thrown across the room, hit a counter and several tables and suffered severe nerve, tissue, and muscle damage to her legs; she spent a month in a wheelchair. Chip ended up in critical condition with 80 stitches in his head and an infection in his lungs. Unable to leave the intensive care unit, he was not able to attend his daughter's first memorial service.

Returning home without Teagan was excruciating. In addition to coming to grips with their own pain and loss, the Ferlaaks were left to explain to Brock why his sister would not be coming home. They tearfully explained over and over that Teagan was in heaven. Young Brock asked time and time again, "How can I get her down?" Wyndham, just six months old, underwent extensive therapy in order to help restore basic functionality and now uses sign language as her only form of communication. The doctors initially told the Ferlaaks that Wyndham would never walk again, but she is a fighter and has proven them wrong.

At the sentencing hearing for Cynthia Kundrat, the judge afforded the Ferlaaks an opportunity to speak their peace. Instead of the tongue-lashing that virtually everyone expected, to the bewilderment of those in the courtroom, the Ferlaaks offered their heartfelt forgiveness to the driver who had destroyed their family. They took the time to methodically articulate the pain and suffering that was inflicted and the nightmares that will forever haunt them, but in an astonishing show of grace, the Ferlaaks made sure to deliver a message of hope.

This was not an easy decision. They had wrestled with it, prayed about it, and asked for guidance. Even though the driver expressed no remorse and never reached out to the Ferlaaks in any way, they offered her their understanding and forgiveness in the courtroom. Throughout the grieving process they had begun to feel sorry for the driver for not having the grounding element of faith that was such an essential part of their lives. They realized how fortunate they were to have experienced any time at all with Teagan and to have that level of awareness.

They made it clear that they would seek the maximum penalty, but in their hearts the Ferlaaks knew that true justice would be found only in healing and forgiveness.

Chip, Jody, Jacqy, and me.

PART THREE

★

BACK TO IRAQ

22.

HELMET FIRE

*We need to find God, and he cannot be found
in noise and restlessness. See the stars,
the moon and the sun, how they move in silence...
We need silence to be able to touch our souls.*

—MOTHER TERESA

Part of the responsibility of an Air National Guard pilot is to be ready when called upon. This can be a difficult transition to make at times, going from tranquil green fairways to the stressful browns of the desert. When the 125th Fighter Squadron goes to war, one of its most important jobs is to perform close air support. We work with the Army and the Marines. If they are in trouble, if they are pinned down by enemy forces, we help them out with strategic strikes.

In 2005, we were flying in support of Operation Iraqi Freedom. We were stationed at the Al Udeid Air Base in Qatar, about 300 miles down the Persian Gulf from Iraq.

I saw the ground in Iraq one time during this entire deployment. We were vampires flying long missions in single-seat fighters at night and sleeping in blacked-out trailers during the day. Each night, as I settled into the cockpit getting ready to start the jet, I said a prayer asking the Lord to keep me safe and give me the physical, emotional, and spiritual strength to overcome the tests that awaited my wingman and me over the next six to eight hours. During our missions we would bear the responsibility of doing everything possible to ensure that the troops on the ground were safe and made it home to their families. One particular night, my second-to-last combat mission of this tour, our job was especially taxing.

It was a typical night in Iraq. Thick dust shrouded the entire country. As my eyes scanned out of the F-16's clear bubble canopy, the sparse lighting of the landscape below was a virtual mirror image of the stars above. Looking out, I couldn't tell which way was up or down. Compounding the lack of visual references is the relatively small amount of seat-of-the-pants sensations you get when flying the F-16. It is such a pure flying machine that at night it can actually feel motionless. The cockpit silence and perfect stability make it a very insidious environment that can turn deadly in seconds. This lack of sensory cues can result in severe spatial disorientation. This is the greatest killer of F-16 pilots. It was in similar conditions that Kevin "Sonny" Sonnenberg lost his life flying in a Tulsa F-16 while taking off into the "black hole," leaving behind his wife, Lindsay, and son, Carson.

On this dangerous night my eyes worked in circles, constantly cross-checking the green-iridescent instrumentation. This is the only reliable reference to keep you alive. Combine these environmental challenges with the dynamic nature of combat and you have the perfect kindling for "helmet fire."

Helmet Fire

"Helmet fire" is a phrase unique to the fighter-pilot community. It describes the moments when your brain is overloaded with more information than it can process. And for me, this was one of those nights. We raced across the ink black skies, having been called on several missions to help Army and Marine forces fighting a deadly ground battle. The pressure pushed me to the edge of my capabilities. The F-16 is a single-seat fighter, but my first instructor pilot Captain Lobash was in the cockpit with me that night, whispering those hallowed words that keep you alive: *Aviate, navigate, communicate.*

By the time we had finished our mission taskings for the night, I had nothing left. I was just plain cooked, courtesy of multiple helmet fires. We finally got fenced out—safeing up our weapons, going from combat mode to navigation mode. We rendezvoused with our tanker buddies for one last sip of gas as we pressed south out of Iraq down the Persian Gulf. I was the flight lead that night, and my wingman Scott "Rookie" Rooks was flying a mile and a half radar-trail behind me. We fly in radar-trail when the environmentals prevent us from flying in a visual formation. As we passed into Kuwaiti airspace, the sky started clearing up. Rookie came over the interflight UHF radio and made a request: "Hey, Noonan... turn down your lights."

"Turn down my lights?" I queried, still trying to decompress from the night's mission.

"Your interior lights," he said. "Turn them down."

With the autopilot engaged, I reached down over my right leg and slowly turned the six dials counterclockwise.

149

The green glow gradually faded in the cockpit until I was engulfed in blackness.

"Okay," I responded, wondering what was up.

"Look up."

My tired eyes peered through the canopy and, in sharp contrast to all of the stress and carnage, my eyes fell upon the most explosive natural display of light I had ever witnessed in my life. There were millions of stars putting on a show. To the west, awash in infinite space blue, the Milky Way was so rich with stars as to emit a frothy quality—it looked like the top of a Starbucks cappuccino.

As I sat, surrounded by the bubble canopy of the F-16 at 31,000 feet, cutting across this miraculous sky, I asked myself, "How is it possible that I was able to go from a place of complete chaos to a place of pure peace so quickly?" Synchronicity had placed me in this perfect moment, I thought of my wife, my daughters, and my parents. How I would love to encapsulate this and share it with them. As I would soon be headed stateside, I began thinking about the soldiers who weren't going home and those severally wounded. War takes everything from a relative few but returns freedom to millions.

It's these moments of intervention in your life when you realize there is a force at work beyond your comprehension. The challenge is to remain present and recognize it. In my case I can trace my calling in life to the time of reflection immediately following that show of starry froth across the heavens. At that moment I knew I had to find a way to help those soldiers who wouldn't make it home from war as well as those forever impacted by the wounds they incurred in combat. Inspiration only matters if you take action. Unfortunately, when the moment of inspiration passed, my eagerness to step up and make a difference quickly slipped to the back of my mind. I didn't think about it for another five months after that sortie in Iraq. I came home to my family and settled back into my daily routine. God had a plan, but I was too distracted to listen. He would use the force of synchronicity to interrupt my life again. Placing me on United 664 with Corporal Brock Bucklin and the death of a fellow F-16 pilot were signs I could not ignore.

Waiting for Daddy to land.

23.

TROJAN

We are here for a reason.

—Major Troy "Trojan" Gilbert

TROJAN
By Ginger Gilbert

There is a snapshot of Troy Gilbert taken when he played Little League baseball. I couldn't help but smile when I looked at him closely in that photo. The team photograph was taken at the baseball field at Laughlin Air Force Base, Texas. That day, all the players but Troy were looking into the camera lens. His eyes were diverted at the sky as jets flew overhead.

Troy was born to be a pilot. The son of a proud military family, he also was a devout Christian, a loving husband, and a devoted father to five children: Boston (age eight at the time of Troy's death), Greyson (then six), Isabella (then three), and twins Aspen and Annalise (then nine months).

He also was a great warrior, having been given the call sign "Trojan" by his fellow fighter pilots. He was someone who lived the sterling example of placing service before self.

This is my story of my late husband, whom I am most grateful to have known since our days in college at Texas Tech University. We met as teenagers and married the week after college graduation.

Perhaps through this reflection you may better know him and the sacrifice he and so many thousands of other men and women have made through the conflicts in Iraq or Afghanistan.

Major Troy "Trojan" Gilbert, a U.S. Air Force F-16 fighter pilot with more than 1,000 flying hours, was stationed at Luke AFB as the 309th Fighter Squadron Assistant Director of Operations. He was deployed to the 332d Air Expeditionary Wing at Balad Air Base, Iraq.

Troy "Trojan" Gilbert.

On November 27, 2006, Major Gilbert led a flight of two F-16s in an aerial combat mission near Tadji, Iraq. On the ground, insurgents were unleashing truck-mounted heavy machine guns, rocket-propelled grenades, small-arms fire, and mortars to attack coalition troops.

In addition, a downed army helicopter crew was in danger of being overrun. Engaging the enemy meant certain antiaircraft fire, but despite the danger, he went after the insurgents.

He launched a strafing attack against the truck, destroying it with his 20-mm Gatling gun. Despite enemy fire, Major Gilbert continued to press the insurgents with a second strafing pass at extremely low altitudes to help save the lives of the helicopter crew and other ground forces while at the same time committing not to harm innocent civilians.

It was during that low second strafing pass that his aircraft hit the ground, and he perished upon impact. His body was never recovered. I later learned that his actions saved 22 lives.

A week after Troy's death, I received a letter with words I will never forget. It was from the army special operations commander of the ground element that Troy saved that day in Iraq.

In keeping with the continued security of the commander and his family, his name is not mentioned here. Yet his words ring loud and clear and speak volumes about a man he never got the chance to meet.

"Our entire ground assault force owes Major Gilbert an unrepayable debt of gratitude for the actions he took that day. Faced with a crisis situation, we were in dire need of air support to fend off an enemy that had us greatly outnumbered and outgunned.

"Trojan responded in a calm, collected manner and exuded professionalism and complete control in this situation. We were in a very vulnerable position on the ground and in great danger of having heavy casualties inflicted upon us. Instead of loitering at high altitudes, Trojan came down on the deck and made it very obvious to the enemy that he was gunning for them.

"They immediately broke their position and began to flee when he started his strafing runs. During these actions, it was obvious to all of us on the ground that he was singlehandedly breaking apart the enemy forces. Simply put, Troy saved us from certain heavy casualties on 27 November. We are forever indebted to Trojan because of the valorous actions he took. None of us will forget his sacrifice, and we will always be humbled with the knowledge that he gave his life in our defense."

Major Gilbert's DNA is laid to rest in Arlington National Cemetery. Troy posthumously earned many awards that day, including the Distinguished Flying Cross with Valor and the Purple Heart.

Major Gilbert's final act of moral and physical courage was conducted selflessly and with honorable bravery. Our American way of life and the security of our country continue, in part, due to Troy's commitment to noble acts on November 27.

They say that there is one percent of the U.S. population in the military. Think of the millions whom that one percent serve. We are indebted to them for their service above self.

As Troy would say, *"We are here for a reason."*

PART FOUR

A PATRIOT'S CALLING

24.

FOLDS OF HONOR

⭐

You can't live a perfect day
without doing something for someone
who will never be able to repay you.

—JOHN WOODEN

Brock Bucklin's homecoming aboard United Flight 664 and Troy Gilbert's death had a profound effect on me. As I see it, my life to that point had been one big training mission for the real thing. It was the culmination of all of my life's experiences and influences. I was not connected to these events by chance—there was a purpose. God had called me on a mission and I was finally prepared to take action. I looked at what was in my power and started from there. After all, everything starts somewhere.

The plan was to share my experiences with the hope that I could create awareness and raise a little money to help the Bucklins and Gilberts. It began with a golf tournament at the Grand Haven Golf Club in Grand Haven, Michigan, a fitting place to start, since that is where I was going on that fateful night.

My idea to use golf to help the families impacted by war was by no means original. Dating back to World War I, golf has been a benevolent friend to our troops. Some of the greatest golfers in our nation, including Bobby Jones, Chick Evans, Walter Hagan, and Francis Quimet, donated their time and talents to raise money for our troops. The United States Golf Association hosted Liberty Tournaments to benefit the Red Cross.

During World War II, the game contributed at even greater levels. The elite clubs across America, typically closed to the public, opened their doors to allow military personnel to play. The Congressional Country Club, outside Washington, D.C., was converted to a training ground for the troops. The famed Augusta National closed in 1942 and was joined by clubs across the nation as they planted gardens, dubbed "victory gardens," to help alleviate food shortages.

Golf greats enlisted in the war effort. Bobby Jones, the only golfer to win four consecutive major championships in the same year (The Grand Slam), actually landed on the beaches of Normandy on June 7, 1944, D-Day plus one, at age 42!

I knew in my heart that golfers were standing by ready to serve; they just needed a call to action. After a few months of soliciting participants and rounding up sponsors, we held the first event, which was the precursor to Patriot Golf Day in August of 2006. The tournament raised a little more than $8,000. We were thrilled to make a donation to help our hurting military families. I slept well, knowing that we could all be proud of our efforts. It was my first true taste of the fulfillment that comes from giving. I discovered one of the infinite treasures in life that day. I learned that when you reach out to someone in need, you are actually the one being helped. It was what Mom had been trying to instill in me by setting the example for me as a young boy. I had figured out a major piece of my quintessence.

Several months later, as we were preparing for the next tournament, I had an idea. This concept, if it worked, could have a substantial and lasting impact: Patriot Golf Day.

The premise was to mobilize golfers on a large scale, similar to that of World War II. We would ask golf courses around the nation to dedicate one day and collect an additional dollar for each of their green fees. I bounced the idea off Jacqy and Dad, and they thought it had potential. Dad has consulted for *Golf Digest* for 20+ years, and we figured that it was an ideal place to pitch Patriot Golf Day. We contacted Roger Schiffman at the magazine, who also thought the idea had promise. He appreciated my spirit and passion. He agreed to feature Patriot Golf Day in *Golf Digest*.

I learned another valuable lesson in a hurry: if you don't have the courage to ask for something, no matter what it is, you won't get it. I asked him if he could drum up additional support for the mission. He made contact with Jim Nantz at CBS Sports.

I remember the day I received an email from Jim. As a sports junkie, I have been a fan of his for many years. His opening line of the Masters is one of my favorite in all of sport: "Hello, friends." So I was floored when Jim pledged support on both a personal level and on behalf of CBS Sports. I began to feel a larger force was piloting this plane. Soon after, CBS Sports agreed to do a segment that included taking the famous golf announcer David Feherty for an F-16 flight. We were going straight vertical, and the afterburner was cooking.

Having secured the support of *Golf Digest* and CBS Sports, I then contacted the PGA of America. The PGA is the world's largest sports organization, with over 27,000 men and women golf professionals. Approximately half of golf courses in America are operated by PGA professionals, and I knew that for Patriot Golf Day to work, we would need the support of the PGA of America.

I reached out to sitting president and fellow PGA member Brian Whitcomb. To my amazement Brian returned my call. He listened intently to my story and inspiration. I quickly found out that Brian is a patriot. He didn't hesitate to answer the call, and he garnered the support of Joe Steranka, the CEO of the PGA. We were getting ready to charge the hill. On our flank we were joined by the United States Golf Association (USGA) and a host of other organizations that supported the cause. The first annual Patriot Golf Day was set for Labor Day weekend in 2007.

It was happening. In just 90 days we put it all together. Sitting in my home office, armed with a one-page email and a cell phone, we mobilized a coalition for Patriot Golf Day. We created a nonprofit organization. Our dream was to form a foundation that would provide scholarships for the spouses

PGA of America President Brian Whitcomb
was one of the first believers and was instrumental
in making the dream of Patriot Golf Day a reality.

and children of our military members who have been killed
or disabled defending the United States of America. As
the son of a college professor, I have witnessed the limitless
power of education. What a wonderful gift to give back to
those military families who have made the ultimate sacrifice
for our freedoms and alleviate a little of the suffering they
have endured.

With the exception of taking a half day for the birth of our
third daughter, I spent virtually every moment working on
Patriot Golf Day. This was a huge undertaking full of major
logistical challenges. There were several days that I wondered
if it was really going to happen. In the end, thanks to the
efforts of the PGA of America team led by Jamie Carbone,
it did.

Our goal was to have 500 golf courses participate in our first year. We had great press coverage from CBS, *Golf Digest*, Golf Channel, Golf Week, CNN, and a host of others. By Labor Day weekend we had over 3,000 golf courses signed up. In 2007 we raised approximately $1 million. The game of golf was yet again supporting our troops!

You probably haven't seen them on TV walking alongside Tiger Woods, but the PGA professionals of the 41 PGA Sections make Patriot Golf Day a success. They are the wingmen deployed at golf courses all across America. They run the facilities that promote Patriot Golf Day, and it is through their efforts that funds are raised to support the Folds of Honor Foundation. The United States Golf Association (USGA), its 900,000-plus members, and golfers across this great nation are the jet fuel that enables Patriot Golf Day fly.

Patriot Golf Day has raised over $40 million and allowed the Folds of Honor Foundation to take flight and distribute over 7,500 scholarships to deserving military families. Even though the enormity of the cause is daunting, we have changed many lives and will continue our efforts, so help me God. Like soldiers on the battlefield, the Folds of Honor Foundation vows to leave no family behind. We are committed to honor, inspire, and empower our military families. If you think about it, we are all military families because we are all free.

The little boy watching his father come home on United Flight 664 was only four at the time. Jacob, now nine, was our first recipient. Awarding Jacob's scholarship was one of the most fulfilling moments in all my life.

Jacob is Coorpal Bucklinsa son
and is our first Scholarship recipient

FOLDS *of* HONOR

www.foldsofhonor.org

25

GOD IS YOUR WINGMAN

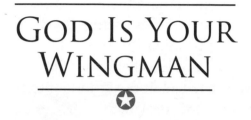

Chance is a word void of sense;
nothing can exist without a cause.

—VOLTAIRE

When people learn that I am a pilot, they often ask me if I have a hard time sitting on a commercial airliner with someone else flying the plane. My reply: "No, because in life I figured out a long time ago that I am not the pilot in command." I firmly believe that there is a higher power in control.

When I do fly commercial, I am almost always on the 6:00 A.M. flight out of Tulsa. One day, however, I opted for the 10:00 A.M. flight so I would not miss my daughter's "Donuts with Dad" celebration at her school. We have no greater gift or responsibility than raising our children, and I do my best to put family first. I left Victoria's school with a smile on my face and a cell phone stuck to my ear. I was working—rather unsuccessfully—to put a team in place to help grow the Folds of Honor Foundation.

Following Patriot Golf Day, we were blessed with the ability to help a few hundred families. But I was in desperate need to build some infrastructure for the Folds of Honor. Despite tremendous support from the PGA of America, the reality that I could not run the foundation alone was quickly setting in. We needed additional funding to hire some patriots to help run the foundation.

While I was checking in at the airport, the gate attendant noticed that I was in the military and gave me an upgrade to first class. *What a nice surprise*, I thought.

At 9:30 A.M. I boarded an American Airlines flight bound for Dallas with continuing service to Grand Rapids. I was still chatting away feverishly on my cell phone as I took my seat. The flight attendant closed the door and gave me that shut your phone off or else look. I said a quick good-bye and as I hung up the man sitting next to me curiously looked over. "What do you do?"

"Do you really want to know?"

"Sure! We have 45 minutes to Dallas…"

"Okay…"

For the next 30 minutes I shared with this stranger my essence, the journey I was on, my resolve to continue to help the families that have given us our freedoms, and my current dilemma: how to build a team at the foundation.

The stranger listened intently, and I could see in his glassy eyes that he was a believer and an excellent man. When I finished sharing my passion, I could hardly believe what this stranger said.

"You are not going to believe this," he began. "My name is Master Sergeant Mike Daggett and I have been hopping around Texas today in order to get my executive platinum status on American Airlines. I am flying eight segments, from San Antonio, to Dallas, to Tulsa, and so on. I'm in Tulsa by chance. I'm not even getting off the airplane. I actually work for the Air National Guard in recruiting and retention, and we just received additional funding to promote Hometown Heroes. Would you be able to come to Washington, D.C., and discuss becoming a part of this mission?"

"Yes!"

As we descended into Dallas/Fort Worth, I noticed a brilliant cloud formation with sunbeams piercing through the bubbling cumulus. It was obvious that someone else was piloting this airplane.

Over the next several months, MSgt Daggett became one of our staunchest supporters. He worked on our behalf with his commanding officers to form a partnership that would supply the much-needed funds to build our team. Despite his best efforts, though, he could not move the colonel off high center until one chance moment at LAX Airport.

Mike was waiting for a flight to Pearl Harbor with the colonel and lobbying on our behalf when at that very moment the colonel glanced at the TV; the Patriot Golf Day PSA was being broadcast. The colonel's reaction was swift; he recognized the synchronicity of the moment. "That is surely a sign that we should be working with Captain Dan! Make it happen."

From this partnership we would receive the funding necessary to take the next steps forward to help our military families.

One vital piece of this puzzle was a man named Major Ed Pulido.

With Master Sgt. Mike Daggett.

26.

SACRIFICE

No man is worth his salt who is not ready
at all times to risk his well-being,
to risk his body, to risk his life, in a great cause.

—THEODORE ROOSEVELT

Operation Iraqi Freedom has required great courage, commitment, and sacrifice by American and coalition forces. The sands of Iraq are stained with the blood of many great patriots.

One of those patriots is my close friend, Edward Pulido. He has been pushed to the edge physically, emotionally, and spiritually by recent events in his life.

On August 17, 2004, Major Pulido of Oklahoma City was well into his third tour of duty in Iraq, a yearlong mission with the Coalition Military Assistance Training Team (CMATT) of the 75th Division of the U.S. Army Reserve, supported by the 1st Calvary Division of Fort Hood, Texas. Major Pulido was traveling in a seven-vehicle convoy from the Tadji Military Training Base northwest of Baghdad to the Kirkuk Military Training Base near the northwestern border of Iran.

Major Pulido was driving an ordinary civilian SUV—no armor plating, no special defenses. These "soft targets" were particularly sought out by insurgents because they often carried high-value targets, i.e., high-ranking officials. Major Pulido's route that day took him straight through the heart of Baghdad. With plenty of tall buildings to perch on and little crevices in which to hide, the bad guys had many places in that city from which they could launch attacks. Convoys that maneuvered through high-traffic areas could regularly expect to contend with snipers' nests, rolling grenades, rocket-propelled grenades (RPGs), and small-arms fire.

After successfully negotiating the crowded streets of Baghdad, Major Pulido and his passengers felt a bit of relief, albeit short-lived. While open spaces are generally less hostile than the confines of cities and towns, the next leg of their journey took them along Highway 5, right into "IED Alley." This corridor is aptly named for the prominence of improvised explosive devices (IEDs) and vehicle borne IEDs (VBIEDs) that have wreaked havoc among coalition forces. As he traveled at about 60 miles per hour, all the while passing craters from previous detonations, Major Pulido's alertness was ratcheted up a couple of notches by fear. He then experienced in slow motion the horror that unfolded as they neared Baqubah.

The sudden blast from the left side of the SUV tossed it from the pavement. The force obliterated nearly every window in the vehicle, littering Major Pulido's face with an infinitesimal number of glass shards. The crushing blow of the airbag pinned his arms to the steering wheel, miraculously enabling him to hold it steady, preventing the vehicle from rolling. With fuel pouring from the gas tank, Colonel Kenneth Stone, riding in the passenger seat and having suffered a concussion, managed to unstrap Major Pulido's seat belt, dislodge him from the airbag, and pull him from the wreckage.

Major Pulido had just borne the brunt of an explosion so powerful that it stripped the hand guards from his M-16 rifle. Lying on the pavement in 128-degree heat in a state of shock, he began looking himself over for damage. His eyes fell upon his leg: unrecognizable, destroyed. In addition to suffering gaping, searing, and shattering wounds to his leg, knee, and pelvis, Major Pulido was riddled with shrapnel in his abdomen, arm, and shoulder. He was bleeding to death on the road.

A combat medic from Nebraska in the SUV that day provided critical support, while the rest of the convoy sprang into action. The four gun trucks that were providing security formed a perimeter around the downed soldier. They stopped all traffic and shielded Major Pulido while awaiting the arrival of the Medivac helicopter.

As Major Pulido lay on the battlefield fighting for breath, the seconds ticked away. He thought of his wife, Karen, and his daughter, Kaitlin, afraid he would never see them again. "What will be done to help my family?" he wondered. Major Pulido was deep in the realm between fear and faith as he waited for 45 minutes before the welcoming thumps of helicopter blades were heard. "God's coming to get me," Major Pulido said to himself. In all, 56 minutes elapsed from the time of the attack to the time he arrived at an emergency hospital. It was there that he finally stopped bleeding and began to realize that he would survive.

Lying in a hospital bed in Baghdad, the horror of the event now behind him, the real challenge began. Major Pulido was first transported to Landstuhl Regional Medical Center in Germany. From there he was flown across the Atlantic and admitted to Walter Reed Medical Center in Washington, D.C. Finally he was taken to Brooke Army Medical Center in San Antonio, Texas, where he received treatment to control the infections that had developed in his knee.

Throughout the course of his treatment, the surgeons were able to extract nearly every piece of debris from Major Pulido's shrapnel-ridden body—all but one. It's a piece he still carries inside him to this day. It was this remaining piece of metal that triggered the infection that would ultimately cost Major Pulido his left leg. Finally, 52 days after the attack, doctors broke the news that they would have to amputate. On October 1, 2004, Major Pulido underwent a 17-hour surgery and six blood transfusions to rid him of the incurable infection that cost him his leg.

He spent 60 days in the hospital; his weight plummeted from 195 to 118 pounds. During his recovery period Major Pulido was visited by General David Petraeus, Commander of Multi-National Security Transition Command–Iraq, who awarded Major Pulido a Purple Heart. General Peter Pace, Vice Chairman of the Joint Chiefs of Staff, also visited Major Pulido. Those visits boosted his morale and provided him some needed perspective. As Ed lay in his hospital bed, General Pace offered hope and purpose: "Always remember that on that day you did not lose your leg. On that day you sacrificed it for your country so all in this nation can be free."

He advanced rapidly through his recovery, but it wasn't easy. He still suffers from post-traumatic stress disorder (PTSD) and phantom pains. The road has been tedious. There were times when he considered giving up after losing his limb. Losing it hurt more than the attack itself. He struggled to believe; his faith in God was tested. He felt hopeless. In fact, he hit rock bottom. They took his leg, but only time would heal his heart. Major Ed embodies the spirit of a warrior.

Major Pulido medically retired from the army on May 16, 2005, after 19 years in uniform. Looking back on his military experience, Major Pulido says that he wouldn't hesitate to do it all over again. He is proud to have sacrificed for the country he loves so much.

I am honored that Major Pulido has joined the Folds of Honor Foundation. No one is more committed to ensuring that the American people honor and invest in our veterans. I am in awe of his character, commitment, honor, and dedication. He has taught me so much about what it means to be a true patriot.

As a small installment on a debt that we will never be able to fully repay, the Folds of Honor Foundation is privileged to have provided scholarships to both Major Pulido's daughter Kaitlin and his latest addition in 2006, daughter Kinsley.

Major Pulido and Karen teach their girls about the gifts they have been given in this great country and that what they have is a result of the sacrifices made by so many over the past

250 years. We must all work hard. We must all contribute to ensure that our way of life is passed on to future generations.

As he was lying on the battlefield that broiling August day in 2004, Major Pulido prayed that he would get the chance to be with his wife again and see his daughter grow up. Thankfully, his prayers were answered.

Major Ed is the brother I never had.

27.

DEPLOYMENT

✪

We make war so that we may live in peace.

—ARISTOTLE

Life before a combat deployment provides brilliant clarity. War puts everything in perspective. In the weeks, days, and hours leading up to a tour of duty, your life is simple, focused on what truly matters—your quintessence. Your true priorities emerge. The people and things that might have taken precedence in the weeks before, such as business meetings, playing golf, checking email, or even watching TV, just don't seem to matter that much anymore. Don't misunderstand—we all have daily routines and responsibilities, but there is nothing like a pending deployment to make you appreciate what is important.

On the eve of my departure for Iraq, the nightly ritual is the same as usual in the Rooney house—dinner, baths, and bedtime stories. My girls don't know it, but their routine is about to change as their daddy will soon step out of their lives, bound for the other side of world. I remind them that Daddy's going on a long trip to help people.

Kids don't understand the concept of war because they are inherently good. Watching their peaceful, rhythmic breathing as they sleep, I give each of them one last kiss before I head off to the base. It never gets any easier to leave your kids. I can't explain it, but anyone who has gone to war understands the separation anxiety. Going to combat is like stepping out of your life. Your life continues without you: soccer games, holidays, birthdays, and other everyday stuff. Few things have had a greater impact on my perspective on life than the three opportunities I have had to give my mortality a quick look in the eyes. Leaving your family, your home, and your life's routine provides a powerful portal to your quintessence.

In the fall of 2008 we were called to deploy in support of Operation Iraqi Freedom. Reporting into the squadron just before midnight, we sat through weather and flight briefs. A few minutes later we stepped to our jets in preparation for a 10-hour flight from Oklahoma to Spain. "Clear to start two, chief?"

"Yes sir, she is ready to go to Spain," replied my crew chief. The crew chief ultimately owns the jets; pilots just borrow them. Crew chiefs are responsible for maintaining every aspect of the F-16. I can't say enough about the men and women who maintain the jets and keep the pilots flying them safe. They are a remarkable group of patriots.

At 0100 I started the jet and slowly closed the canopy. The warm cockpit lit by the iridescent green lights would be my home for the next 11 hours. No in-flight movies, no getting up to stretch your legs, just me and God.

Deployment

At precisely 0200, the 15 foot-long fire of the afterburner lit up the night, preempting the ascent of the powerful F-16. One after another, separated by 20 seconds, the fire-breathing beasts pointed toward the galaxies. Flames scorched the air as the 125th Fighter Squadron woke up Tulsa with the deafening sound of freedom. As I focused intently on the mission ahead, Jacqy cried softly as she stood in the backyard and listened to my goodbye fade into the distant sky.

Like all fighters, the F-16's greatest weakness is its limited range. The jet is built for speed and breaking the bad guys' stuff. Its sleek design doesn't allow for much fuel capacity. The fuel limitations, like all problems, cease to be a problem once you have a solution. Our solution was about a hundred miles outside of Tulsa. I spotted the set of blinking lights in the distance from our airborne Texaco Station. The silhouette gradually revealed itself, with the help of our night-vision goggles (NVGs), as a KC-135 Stratotanker. Intercepting at 350 knots, all six fighters rejoined on Sting 21's wing. We were now along for the long ride to Spain. The official term is "chicks in tow." As the country slept under a blanket of freedom, the constellation Liberty cut across the starlit sky flashing red and green.

I smoothly flew my F-16 to the stern of the tanker in preparation for my first air refueling. "Two's stabilized pre-contact ready."

The tanker boomer relays, "Two, you're cleared contact."

Like a father with his daughter, I initiated a dance based on utter and complete trust. A small red light that illuminated the end of the refueling boom was my only reference in the

181

dark sky as I flew underneath the KC-135. My full-service attendant, the boomer, lay on his stomach 15 feet above me, peering out a window in the back of the refueler while flying the boom within inches of my jet. His mission was to latch the wing-like air refueling probe into the receptacle on the spine of the F-16.

I hovered without relative motion beneath the massive jet…waiting…"Clunk." I felt the contact and glanced down over my right knee to confirm that the fuel gauge was inching clockwise. It was now up to me to lead this 10-minute dance by making constant corrections in pitch and power to stay connected at 310 knots. There is a light bar on the belly of the tanker that provides the immediate corrections—up, down, forward, aft—to help me keep the jet in the refueling envelope. There is a lot of pressure. If you separate, termed "falling off the boom," you're going to have to buy a round for the boys!

As a young aviator I found air refueling the F-16 the most nerve-racking experience. It is very unnatural to get that close to an enormous jet, let alone intentionally run into it at high speed. It took a couple years, but I gradually became more accustomed to our airborne Texaco partners in the sky. Growth is one of life's greatest rewards when you push yourself. Once you stretch yourself you never go back. I never air-refueled without marveling at the precision and trust required to fight and win. Yet another powerful demonstration that you can't do it by yourself. Your life, like an F-16 crossing the ocean, will never reach its destination without the help from people along the way.

We refueled nine times during our transatlantic crossing. That kept us pretty busy, but the flight was long enough to steal some time soaking up the view. As the sun began to rise I marveled at the razor-sharp transition on the distant horizon as the light-blue sky united with the midnight-blue North Atlantic. *That is the edge of life*, I thought to myself.

Air refueling over the Atlantic on the way to Iraq.

When we completed our last refueling, we said thanks to our tanker buddies and got our own clearance into Spain. Fighters are built for speed. We pushed the throttle forward and were instantly free from the purgatory of 310 knots and shortly on the ground at Morón Airbase in Spain. As I slowly raised my canopy, I was greeted by a fresh Mediterranean breeze. I took a long shower and then headed toward downtown Seville with the boys for our last night of fun before we departed for Iraq.

Forty-eight hours later, climbing out of Spain, I watched the last peaceful sunrise as it lit up the horizon over the Mediterranean Sea. This leg of our journey could have been documented on the History Channel. Our contrails left a signature in the sky above Mount Etna, Greece, the Nile, the Egyptian Pyramids, the Red Sea, and the desolate deserts of Saudi Arabia. During the nine-hour flight into the war zone of Iraq, I reflected on the blessings of the free world. Freedom is like most things in life: you don't truly appreciate it until it's gone.

Most U.S. citizens pledge allegiance to the flag, but the U.S. military is comprised of a small group of volunteers committed to defending the flag.

As we crossed into Iraq, I noticed that the skies had turned brown. I could feel the grit on my teeth as the jet ingested the sand through their oxygen system. The casual conversation on the radio became quiet as the seriousness of the mission began to set in. We were going to war.

Make no mistake; war is an awful thing. There is nothing glamorous about it. You witness the unthinkable. The sights, sounds, and smells of combat are forever burned into your soul. I don't think anyone wants to go to war. You do it for love of country. You do it because you feel compelled to give back to a country that has given so much to you. We trust our President and Congress to run this country and to decide when military force is necessary. When we get the order to go to war, we don't ask questions, but we do ask that they give us the resources and freedom to accomplish our mission.

"Incoming! Incoming!" came the claxon-blared warning of an imminent attack as we pulled our jets into post-flight de-arming. I watched as the soldiers on the ground took cover in the sandbag bunkers. This attack turned out to be a false alarm but it was foreshadowing of what was to come. We would bear the brunt of many attacks during our all-inclusive stay at Joint Base Balad. Located approximately 60 miles northeast of Baghdad, it was nicknamed "Mortaritaville" for the barrage of mortars and rockets lobbed at us by insurgents. Their attacks were unguided and most often missed their marks. But several soldiers have been severely wounded or killed by the "golden-bb." An annoying level of stress was always present, reminding you to stay vigilant. When the base's warning system sounded, I hit the deck, said a quick prayer, and thought skinny.

During our deployment we flew as part of the 332d Expeditionary Squadron. The 332d has a rich and distinguished history. The Tuskegee Airmen who flew their red-tailed P-51s during World War II were epic members of the 332d Fighter Group. These men didn't just fly airplanes; they blazed a trail. They were tested by the enemy and by their fellow Americans. They overcame great social barriers as the first African-American pilots. They pushed the envelope of life. The 332d was the only escort squadron to go the duration of the war without losing any of the B-17 bombers they flew to protect. As interim members of this historic war-fighting tradition, we flew hundreds of F-16 missions in support of Operation Iraqi Freedom. It was an honor to serve as a member of the Red Tails.

The 332d was meaningful for another reason. It's the same squadron Major Troy "Trojan" Gilbert was flying out of when he perished in 2006. The base was full of reminders of this great man and those he touched. I often thought of Troy as I visited the Gilbert Memorial Chapel for daily Catholic Mass. The efforts of Troy and thousands of other soldiers have paved the way for a brighter future in Iraq. Great progress virtually always requires great sacrifice.

By the fall of 2008, Iraq had made tremendous gains, and many regions were stabilizing. However, violence persisted. Casualties were still occurring on a nearly daily basis. When I was not flying a mission, I spent time volunteering at the hospital. Balad has the most sophisticated trauma hospital in the world. Wounded soldiers who make it to Balad with a pulse have a 98-percent chance of survival. This is sharp contrast to wars of the past and why we have so many disabled veterans coming home. As I walked the halls of the hospital, the smell of trauma was a reminder of the horrible reality of combat. The doctors and nurses cared for U.S. forces, Iraqis, and insurgents with equal regard—a testament to the character and virtue of the United States of America.

28.

COMBAT LETTER

★

Love is composed of a single soul
inhabiting two bodies.

—ARISTOTLE

Throughout history, soldiers have written letters to be passed on to their loved ones in the event that they didn't make it home. I wrote this letter before my third tour. I share in the hopes of providing some perspective on the sacrifice all military families are prepared to make in defense of our nation.

Date: 5 Sept 2008

Dear Jacqy,

As I thought of what to write to you in this letter, I remembered an encounter we had a few years back. Most people would call it chance, but you and I both know there is no such thing as chance.

I remembered an evening when we trekked on the banks of a cove along the shore of Lake Michigan. We were having a conversation about nothing, one of my favorite things to do with you, by the way, when that old man emerged. He had a soft smile on his brown and weathered face. "I've been watching you," he said. As he turned his gaze toward the lake, I could see tears welling in his eyes. His lip quivered. "My wife passed away two months ago. I can see the love you have for each other, and it reminds me of the love my wife and I shared. We spent 57 years together, and now the Lord has taken her from me."

He turned back to us with a reminder: "Love each other and enjoy every moment together, because it seems like only yesterday that my wife and I were walking on this very beach, just like you two, our whole lives ahead of us."

As I remembered this, Jacqy, I thought about our lives... both the good times and the times we were tested. They were all part of the journey and part of what made our commitment and marriage so strong.

It seemed like yesterday that I first saw you at the Sigma Chi House. You were so different than all the other girls. I had never met anyone with a smile so infectious. You were so positive, and you laughed all the time. We never stopped laughing.

If I have one complaint, it's that time passes too quickly when we are together. I can't believe it has been 17 years. I wish I could have frozen our lives in time. Our parents are healthy, the kids are happy, and in their eyes we are still the coolest people in the world... at least for a couple more years anyway.

There is no doubt that together we could get through anything. You were my foundation, always there to lend a hand or advice. The milk for my low-fat Oreos. My motivation to get a little bit better every day.

Your unconditional support gave me the courage to dream big. Regardless of how difficult the day, I always knew that it would be all right when I got home. As I walked through the front door, regardless of how crazy things were, you'd stop and take five seconds to give me a kiss.

Thank you for being my wife. Thank you for allowing me to be me. Thank you for steering me through the difficult times…you always had just the right words, even when I was the one being difficult. Thank you for waking up happy every morning. Thank you for keeping me young and sharing my passion for life.

It was amazing how we were always on the same wavelength…although you do like reality TV? I was never able to understand that? You figured out life, and I was playing catch up with you from the day we met. You never lost touch with the little kid in you. You're always giggling… just thinking of your laugh makes me smile. I loved giving you presents because you appreciate even the tiniest gesture. Most of all, I just enjoy hanging out with you. The simplest moments chilling out in the evenings, watching the kids play in the driveway. My favorite place on earth.

Jacqy, you are an amazing mother. I was always in awe watching you take care of our little girls. While I helped, you were doing most of the work, ensuring that our girls had the foundation for a good life. They are growing up in a safe and positive environment..

The last few years working together on the foundation were awesome. It was wonderful to share the experience of true giving with you. I couldn't think of a better example to set for our children or a better way to give back to a country that has given us so many opportunities.

I want you to know that I checked out doing what I loved to do. I will miss you so much. I will miss waking up on Saturday mornings, washing the cars, and watching football together. I miss our long walks and lazy vacations. I miss our exercise dates…isn't it funny how our best times didn't cost anything?

Please don't let the girls forget their dad, and teach them about me as they get older. Keep the legend alive of the roller-coaster man, freeze monster, and the wolf. Leave pictures out and share stories. Please have them pray for me every day. Give them hugs and kisses from their dad. Tell them I said, "Dream big!" Teach them about volition. Challenge them to use their time and talents to positively impact the world.. Let them know how much I love them and that I am always in their hearts. During their toughest times I will be there to give them strength. I will be with them on their wedding days.

Above all else, I want you to be happy. Never stop laughing, and keep smiling. Your happiness is your greatest blessing. Know that I will always be with you. You saved me, and I will be with you to return the favor. I am so sorry I will miss the rest of the journey. Always know that I will be in your heart and that I will be watching over you.

I love you to infinity.

—*Dan*

PART FIVE

LITTLE VOICE

29.

THE PATRIOT

⭐

The soul never thinks without a picture.

—ARISTOTLE

When I received a last-minute invitation to play in a charity tournament from Trey Hawes, a fellow Sigma Chi from the University of Kansas, I initially declined. I already had several appointments on my calendar for that day. As I hung up the phone, however, I had a strange feeling that I was making a mistake. I listened to that little voice and cleared my schedule for that afternoon. Synchronicity was about to change my path again.

It was a perfect Friday in July. A light southerly breeze was blowing, and a few puffy white cumulous clouds were dotting the sky. By chance I was paired with David Charney, who was also a last-minute addition to the group. As we walked and talked that afternoon, we discovered that we had a lot in common. Not only were we both passionate about golf, a game introduced to us by our fathers, but we also had a shared interest in building things.

David described a unique and ambitious project he was spearheading. At over 3,000 acres, complete with a new elementary school, a 100-acre lake, a walking trail system, and a boutique downtown, Stone Canyon was by far the largest and most ambitious master-planned community in Oklahoma history. After I shared my family's experience in golf-course development, David mentioned that he had a wonderful piece of virgin soil, perfect for golf, tucked on the south side of Stone Canyon. Northwest Oklahoma typically offers parkland golf. While enjoyable, it's characteristically gradually rolling terrain, parallel fairways, and just a smattering of trees. Despite my initial lack of optimism, Dad and I decided to go out and look at the land.

Having had the great fortune of playing a number of exceptional courses both here and abroad, I have seen a lot of dirt. "Dirt" is the business term we use to describe the land, and this dirt was unlike anything I had ever seen. I was in awe of the incredible diversity of the terrain: upland prairies, woodlands, canyons, and lowlands. Virtually every topography in Oklahoma was encompassed in 200 acres. I had never seen a golf-course site with four distinct and dramatic environments, and no way would I have expected to see it in Owasso located on the outskirts of Tulsa. With gorgeous sheer limestone rock cliffs, spring-fed stone-bottomed creeks, waterfalls, caves, and meadows, there was no question that this land was sewn together by a higher power.

The memory of life's defining moments never seems to fade. As my father and I stood on the edge of a limestone cliff, we watched the fireflies dancing in the canyons and the lights of Tulsa shimmering on the distant horizon. At that moment,

Dad and I felt a calling to take action. It reminded us of one of our favorite movies Field of Dreams. Ray Kinsella is called by a godlike voice to build a baseball diamond in a cornfield in rural Iowa. While our land was certainly more dramatic than Ray's cornfield, we heard the same calling: "Build it, and they will come." We both agreed that this was a calling that we could not ignore. We would build it. We would call it "The Patriot."

There are no coincidences. Synchronicity is guiding our lives. The key is being present, open, and having the courage to listen to our instincts. Dad and I were certainly aware of the risks. He taught me at a young age that a life without fear is a life that is not being lived to the fullest.

This raw landscape could be entrusted to only the most-capable hands. We contacted the man whom we consider to be the best golf-course architect in the world, Robert Trent Jones, Jr. He has designed more than 245 courses around the globe that span over 40 countries and five continents; the sun literally never sets on the legacy of Robert Trent Jones, Jr. I explained to Bobby and his team that we needed someone to help us create our field of dreams. He laughed and agreed to come have a look at our cornfield.

This land had a similar spiritual impact on Bobby. He saw the potential and felt the calling. The RTJII team quickly agreed to join our mission: "Architects from around the world would shoot it out at the O.K. Corral for the chance to bring The Patriot to life."

After an 11-month negotiation and design process, we got the green light from David and his partners Pete Kourtis,

Greg Simmons, and Bill Atherton. I remember that day vividly. I was thrilled, but my excitement was tempered with trepidation as I knew I was about to embark on one of the most challenging endeavors of my life. I knew that we would be tested physically, emotionally, and spiritually. Learning to fly the F-16 had been an incredibly demanding experience, but making The Patriot dream a reality would be equally challenging in different ways. Known and unknown challenges lie ahead as we embarked on this daunting climb.

I am not a natural-born salesman. In fact, it is one of my least favorite things to do. I had to push myself every day. Over the years I have found that this is a prerequisite when it comes to chasing big dreams. It's like ascending into high altitude: if you can handle the initial decrease in oxygen, you will eventually acclimate. I was hypoxic before I started getting my phone calls and emails returned about The Patriot. My typical day consisted of making cold calls and all too often just leaving messages. The people I did speak with generally said "no," but I kept climbing. While I was certainly tempted to retreat, I never did. Getting repeatedly rejected was the hardest part, but faith was my shield.

In order to commence construction, we needed to sell 35 founding memberships. I gave tours to prospective members several times a week. Over the course of six months I had many people tell me in so many words that I was crazy. I banged up my wife's Pathfinder and infested our house with ticks on two different occasions. But during my nightly de-ticking ritual I stayed positive. With every "no," I reminded myself that I was that much closer to a "yes." It was simply a game of percentages. With persistence and hard work, I began generating some interest—and eventually a few believers.

In Field of Dreams, after Ray finished turning his cornfield into a baseball diamond, his calling became clear. Ecstatic, Ray brought his friends to show them the baseball legends of the past as they appeared out of the corn to play on his field of dreams. Yet only "the believers" could see the game; the rest saw only an empty baseball diamond.

I witnessed a similar phenomenon as I took people on tours of the raw land that would become The Patriot. While some saw it, most were completely oblivious. Like the prune-eating blue hairs on the 747 flight I had ecstatically told I would be a pilot, many of these prospective members gave me patronizing pats on the head. I am the first to concede to these "nonbelievers" that building The Patriot was not a completely rational decision. I refused to let them get me down. I understood that most people would not understand our passion, so it was going to be up to me to keep the fire of my dreams burning. It was a dream fueled by possibility—the possibility of creating a truly special place, a place beyond the ordinary. In my heart I knew that if we could turn our vision into a reality, the believers would come from far and wide. Just like old Terrance Mann told Ray Kinsella, "They'll come to Iowa for reasons they can't even fathom. They'll turn up not knowing for sure why they're doing it. They'll pass over the money without even thinking about it: for it is money they have and peace they lack." As each day passed, we gained a deeper understanding that our pursuit was much deeper then constructing a golf course.

In my experience, if you believe, if you visualize yourself succeeding, you can bring that reality into your life. Self-actualization is a powerful force. I held on tight to the image of mobilizing the 35 founding members, their golf balls taking flight off the first tee, towering nearly 200 feet above the fairway, with the sound of birds and the smell of freshly cut grass. I never stopped believing. I had faith and eventually these visions became reality.

I could see my breath on that cold January morning as I sat quietly on a rock, watching the first grease-mired bulldozer fire up its engine. The black smoke was silhouetted against the grey sky as that tree assassin starting mowing down the future fairways. It was a momentous day.

Robert Trent Jones, Jr., Jay Blasi, and Bruce Charlton did an amazing job with the design of The Patriot. We watched mesmerized as they listened intently to the land just as a father listens to a young child. Patiently and gently they uncovered a golf experience that would become like no other.

As we traversed the four distinct and often-hostile topographies, we were tested. The rock-laden terrain required the importation of 10 inches of sandy-loam topsoil across the entire course. The underground irrigation system was literally carved out of the limestone. The building process took over two years and presented huge challenges for the country's finest golf-construction company, Landscapes Unlimited.

I thought there was nothing that could ruin my first day back from my third tour of duty in Iraq, but I was wrong. Upon my return, I learned that the cost to build The Patriot had escalated by nearly 50 percent. These overruns were occurring at the precise time the second great depression hit. Dad and I had to raise substantial dollars in 90 days or be forced to suspend construction. Despite the dire circumstances, we survived, thanks to a group of believers: David Bond, Eddy Gibbs, Sanjay Meshri, Tom Russell, and Paul Sisemore. Without these great men The Patriot would have likely never have been finished. It was yet another demonstration of how the universe conspires to help those who take risks, chase dreams, and live in the realm between fear and faith.

Rickie Fowler, me, Dad, Tom Russell,
and Paul Sisemore at The Patriot Cup.

Eventually, 80 acres of Meyer zoysia sod brought the enormous fairways to life. With no rough, the fairways are like harbors providing safe havens from nature's fury. The tees and greens were gently laid in the organic contours of the land. The brilliant beach-white sand bunkers sprinkled throughout The Patriot provide a striking contrast to the lush, green zoysia. Emulating life, The Patriot is a blend of penal, strategic, and heroic puzzles that are there for each of us to solve, often by determining the best position from which to attack. The shot values soar off the chart with each hole echoing its own quintessence. The sound of spring-fed limestone streams, waterfalls, wildlife, and bald eagles complete the notes of this epic symphony. "The Patriot was born from the land but is for the spirit," said my good friend Robert Trent Jones, Jr.

I have always been fascinated by the type of people who climb Everest. There is an area near the summit of Everest that is notoriously dangerous. It's known as the "death zone" for the number of fatalities that occur above 26,000 feet. Ten weeks from the course's opening, the skies over Tulsa opened up. The result was a hundred-year flood. The Patriot was trapped in the death zone and devastated.

Just days before, I had been walking the perfectly sodded fairways and marveling at the nearly completed project. Now fairways, greens, bridges, and equipment were destroyed. On the evening of May 1, 2009, I stood on the first tee and was overcome by a feeling of nausea. Looking down at a river that used to be the number-one fairway, I literally struggled to breathe, but I knew in my heart that we had only one option. Just like Fritzie taught me that fateful day on Red Lake, we took off our boots and started bailing. The damage delayed the opening by 11 months, which severely tested us. But once again we survived. It was painful and hard but we persevered.

Looking back, I can see the path of our ascent very clearly. I can see where we struggled and where we occasionally slipped back along the way. As committed and resolute father, son, and friends pursuing a shared dream, we are reminded once again that anything is possible in this country. I learned about the courage to pursue your dreams, the perseverance to make them happen, and how to dig yourself out when you are hit by an avalanche. Failure is necessary for growth, discovery, and success. After all, it's failure only if you fail to learn and evolve.

I can't pinpoint the moment, but somewhere along the way The Patriot became more than just a golf course. The Patriot became part of our quintessence. Dr. Archibald "Moonlight" Graham describes it best in *Field of Dreams*: "This is my most special place in all the world. Once a place touches you like this, the wind never blows so cold again. You feel for it, like it was your child."

It's especially meaningful that The Patriot has been a family affair. What a great reward it is watching Dad play with his grandchildren on the field of dreams we built with our great friends. I know he is proud of me, and I couldn't have done it without his help. It culminated on Memorial Day 2010, when I watched Dad drive the first golf ball at The Patriot. It was a shot that sailed into the ages and initiated a rich tradition on a course that will serve as a reminder to all those who walk its fairways and putt its greens that we are positively blessed to be Americans.

In the closing scene of *Field of Dreams,* Ray's dad emerges from the cornfield to play catch with his son. As they toss the baseball back and forth, Ray asks his dad, "Is there a heaven?"

"Oh yeah, son...it's the place dreams come true."

Taking flight at the 1st tee of The Patriot.

THE
PATRIOT

www.patriotgolfclub.com

The Patriot

Rated in #48 GolfWeek's Top 100 Golf Courses in America (build after 1960)

Rated as GolfWeek's #5 on Top 100 Residential Courses in America

Host of The Patriot Cup

Top New Private Course in America 2010-2011 GolfWeek

Number 2 New Course built in America 2010-2011 GolfWeek

THE
PATRIOT
CUP

www.thepatriotcup.com

30

THE SIXTH FOLD

★

The momentum of freedom in our world is unmistakable—and it is not carried forward by our power alone. We can trust in that greater power Who guides the unfolding of the years. And in all that is to come, we can know that His purposes are just and true.

—GEORGE W. BUSH

On a rainy night in February of 2009, I shared our mission during a gathering of Associated Builders and Contractors at Freddie's Steakhouse in Sapulpa Oklahoma. On behalf of the Folds of Honor, an incredible demonstration of patriotism was launched. Four general contractors—Crossland, Flintco, Key, and LD Kerns—joined with a coalition of subcontractors eventually donating virtually 100 percent of their time and materials to build the Folds of Honor headquarters. A coalition of donors lead by Robert Trent Jones II donated the remaining funds required to finish the building. The Folds of Honor Foundation headquarters sits adjacent to the clubhouse at the Patriot, symbolizing the bond between the two organizations. ABC and its leaders Carl Williams,

Sally Singer, and Barb Risenhoover continue to be tremendous supporters of our military families in need.

The great patriots of ABC.

At 1300 each day at The Patriot, the foundation bell tolls 13 times in reverence to the 13 folds of the flag. It's a special time when everyone takes pause, and in the silence their heart remembers the men and women who serve and have served this nation. It also is a reminder to all that we are called to give back to our country.

The Patriot is more than a golf course; it's a symbol. It stands as a testament to our freedoms and to the enduring fabric of this great nation. It combines God, Country, and the Game. We are a band of brothers living in one nation under God without apology. We are the first to stand and last to sit down.

It is a special place built to inspire and revitalize patriotism. Each hole pays tribute and carries the name of a great patriot, including George Washington, Martin Luther King, the Wright Brothers, and Dwight D. Eisenhower, to name a few. On quiet evenings, if you listen closely, you will hear the hearts of great patriots echoing in the canyons.

The American flag is folded 13 times to achieve its triangular shape. After the flag is completely folded and tucked in, it takes on the appearance of a cocked hat, reminding us of the soldiers who served under General George Washington.

Each fold has a specific definition. The Folds of Honor Foundation was inspired by the sixth fold.

- The first fold of our flag is a symbol of life.

- The second fold is a symbol of our belief in eternal life.

- The third fold is made in honor and remembrance of the veterans departing our ranks who gave a portion of their lives for the defense of our country to attain peace throughout the world.

- The fourth fold represents our weaker nature, for as American citizens trusting in God, it is to Him we turn in times of peace as well as in time of war for His divine guidance.

🏴 The fifth fold is a tribute to our country, for in the words of Stephen Decatur, "Our country, in dealing with other countries, may she always be right; but it is still our country, right or wrong."

🏴 The sixth fold is for where our hearts lie. It is with our heart that we "pledge allegiance to the flag of the United States of America, and to the Republic for which it stands, one Nation under God, indivisible, with Liberty and Justice for all."

🏴 The seventh fold is a tribute to our Armed Forces, for it is through the Armed Forces that we protect our country and our flag against all her enemies, whether they be found within or without the boundaries of our republic.

🏴 The eighth fold is a tribute to the one who entered into the valley of the shadow of death, that we might see the light of day, and to honor mother, for whom it flies on Mother's Day.

🏴 The ninth fold is a tribute to womanhood; for it has been through their faith, their love, loyalty, and devotion that the character of the men and women who have made this country great has been molded.

🏴 The tenth fold is a tribute to the father, for he, too, has given his sons and daughters for the defense of our country since they were first born.

🏴 The eleventh fold, in the eyes of a Hebrew citizen, represents the lower portion of the seal of King David and King Solomon, and glorifies in their eyes, the God of Abraham, Isaac, and Jacob.

🏴 The twelfth fold, in the eyes of a Christian citizen, represents an emblem of eternity and glorifies, in their eyes, God the Father, the Son, and Holy Spirit.

🏴 When the flag is completely folded, the stars are uppermost, reminding us of our nation's motto, "In God We Trust."

31.

PROMISE

Faith is a living, daring confidence in
God's grace, so sure and certain that a man
could stake his life on it a thousand times.

—MARTIN LUTHER KING

Building The Patriot was personally fulfilling from many perspectives. In the process I learned more about myself, more about life, and more about people. The Patriot brought some amazing people into my life. Sanjay "Sunny" Meshri is one of those special people who has a positive impact on everyone blessed to know him. Ironically it's a member of an immigrant family from India who has proven to be one of the greatest patriots and greatest friends to my family.

The Meshri family story is the prototypical example of the infinite possibilities afforded in the United States. It's what our men and women in uniform continually fight to protect. It's the best that America has to offer.

We celebrate diversity in this country. Dad encouraged me to discover from an early age, through our travels, that all people possess exceptional gifts. The United States offers the chance for all newcomers to manifest them. We offer hope, we offer inspiration, and we offer opportunity. As is always the case when it comes to giving, the one acting out of benevolence is actually the greatest beneficiary. The Meshris are not only an example of what can be achieved in the United States by hard work and dedication, they are also the perfect illustration of how different cultures add immeasurable value to our society.

Like mine, Sunny's journey began with the special influence of his parents. Married in 1966, Sunny's parents were natives of India who came to America to pursue their dreams. In 1986, Sanjay's dad, Dr. Dayal Meshri, sought to acquire a loan to fund his dream. He wanted to own and operate his own business. He started by asking his friends, and after he exhausted that avenue he moved on to banks. Facing skepticism due to the economic climate at the time, he was rejected, but he kept driving forward and would not give up. Eventually he found Stillwater National Bank. They believed in his vision, and they believed in him. Dr. Meshri was granted a loan of $100,000.

He quickly put this capital to use by purchasing an old, dilapidated 3,000 square-foot building in the Tulsa Port of Catoosa and went to work cleaning it up. Advance Research Chemicals, Inc. (ARC) was launched as a two-person operation. Money was tight, but when Dayal landed a big contract with General Motors, his business took flight. Today, ARC produces over 300 chemicals and conducts business with more than 200 of the Fortune 500 companies across numerous industries. They operate on a global scale with plants in

Mexico and India. Dr. Meshri consistently reminds Sunny, "We work so hard to provide opportunities to the people who work with us." Sunny listened. He started in the family business, working for $18,000 a year. Sunny seized this opportunity and is currently the executive vice president and managing director. This father-and-son duo has taken ARC to new heights.

Anything is possible in this country, and Sunny helped me see this truth more clearly. He is known for his business savvy and drive, but it's his special willingness to listen to others that is the true source behind his uncanny ability to solve problems. Sunny has taught me about listening, being compassionate, the art of business, and making the world a better place. We work together to pay tribute to the men and women who ensure our way of life. We do this on behalf of all who benefit from the promise of America.

Celebrating life with my bro Sanjay.

213

32.

CARPE DIEM
✪

*I believe every human has
a finite number of heartbeats.
I don't intend to waste any of mine.*

—NEIL ARMSTRONG

It started with a call from a good friend of mine, fellow PGA professional Greg Nichols. "Noonan, how'd you like to come over to Hawaii in January and give a couple of talks about the Folds of Honor at the Sony Open?"

Hmm…Let me think…25 degrees and snowing in Tulsa…75 degrees and sunny in Honolulu….

"Yeah, I guess I can make it."

But there was another reason I decided to make the trip, and it goes a little deeper than balmy weather. It has to do with making the most of every second we are afforded on earth. That is what God intended and why every soldier makes sacrifices to preserve our way of life.

As I mentioned earlier, a few movies have had a profound impact on my life. They have the power to entertain, teach, and inspire. *Dead Poets Society* provided a powerful vector toward my quintessence. It's about a group of young students at a New England prep school encouraged by an unorthodox professor to learn, through poetry, how to dream big. As Thoreau said, "…to live deep and suck out all the marrow from life…and not, when I came to die, discover that I had not lived." Put another way by Robert Herrick, "Gather ye rosebuds while ye may, old time is still a flying, and this same flower that smiles today, tomorrow will be dying."

The most moving and inspirational scene in the film for me was when Professor Keating, played by Robin Williams, gathers his impressionable young students in front of a trophy case. It's filled with memorabilia from days gone by and black-and-white photographs from former students. Just like them, they were full of hopes and dreams and in the prime of their lives but they are now "fertilizing daffodils." He asks the students to lean in closely, look into their eyes, and listen to their voices from beyond, "*Carpe Diem.* Seize the day boys… make your lives extraordinary."

This sentiment, that we all have a limited amount of time on this earth and that tomorrow is guaranteed to no one, is the philosophy that Jacqy and I try to inspire our girls with and live our own lives by. We are kindred spirits in that regard. With that in mind, we seized the opportunity to "suck the marrow from life" and packed our bags for the tropical island paradise of Hawaii to tackle our bucket list of "must dos." Skydiving, which held a spot near the top of our list, was about to be crossed off.

My Tuesday speech was scheduled for the Junior Skills Challenge, featuring Steve Stricker, Jerry Kelly, Dean Wilson, and Tad Fujikawa. I would be kicking off the event for the Sony Open, and about a thousand people were expected to attend. But the crowd was anticipating a skills challenge, not a surprise attack from 8,000 feet.

Arriving at Pearl Harbor around noon, I was introduced to my host for the day, Skydive Hawaii. Meeting the demonstration team was like stepping into the movie *Point Break*—none of them were wearing shoes, and all of them greeted me with the "shaka" (hang-loose sign). "Ready to get some air?"

"I think so…" I said, not exactly inspired with confidence.

I would soon find out that the experience level and professionalism of the Skydive Hawaii team doesn't match their casual appearance. Collectively, the group has over 100,000 jumps. They have filmed movies and trained the Special Forces. Still, our demonstration was not atypical jump. In the world of dropping bombs, we classify such maneuvers as "danger close." That is when you have to hit the target precisely because of the risk of collateral damage. In this case we would be landing on the 18th green in a heavily populated area filled with grandstands—though in hindsight I suppose you could do a lot worse than death by Budweiser stand.

In a fighter pilot-like fashion, the team briefed us on the jump. They discussed time and altitude deconfliction, wind direction, and jump location. They covered the possible emergencies and the landing time of exactly 2:55 P.M. And finally they went over the filming of the jump. A team of three dedicated jumpers with high-definition cameras mounted on their helmets were tasked with capturing the event.

"Great," I joked. "If this goes wrong, I'm going to end up on *Faces of Death.*"

Richard, a veteran of 16,000 jumps, briefed me on procedure as we hopped on our ride, a Cessna Caravan all done up in a Hawaiian paint scheme. Taking off, we soaked in the brilliance of the islands. The visibility was so good that you could see Maui.

As we arrived over the jump zone, we still had 15 minutes to loiter over the target. The jump door was opened, and the team motioned for me to look at the golf course below. This was the first time I started getting nervous. No turning back.

"Five minutes!"

The Skydive Hawaii team dutifully prepared us for the jump. They focused on the task at hand while still managing to ease the tension by slipping in a timely remark: "Remember, safety third!" shouted team leader J.C. The jumpers made last-minute safety checks, lowered their goggles, placed their hands one on top of another, and repeated their mantra. "Let's get some air!

"Ten seconds!"

The first four jumpers got into place, and in an instant they were gone. I caught myself struggling to breathe from a combination of nerves and the thin air at altitude. One of the many lessons I have learned over the years is that being brave does not mean you are not afraid—a sentiment that came in handy when staring out an open door in the sky and just seconds from jumping out of a perfectly good airplane.

Climbing into the doorway, I clutched the rail and was literally hanging out the side of the plane. It was sort of like standing backward on a diving board getting ready to do a back flip, only instead of springing three feet into the air and splashing into a warm pool, I was on the verge of hurtling 8,000 feet straight to the ground.

And then I was flying.

Screaming toward the earth at 120 miles per hour. One flip. Another flip. Hands out. Back arched. Wind rushing, speed thrilling. An intoxicating mixture of fear and faith. Suddenly my eyes catch a blue streak. J.C. is chasing me down. He looks like the Terminator with his helmet-cam. Slamming on the breaks, he stops within three feet, staying in formation for the rest of the free fall.

As we approach 4,500 feet, the 18th green is getting big very fast. Let's pray it works. The moment of truth.

Opening shock. J.C. disappears toward Wialea. Looking up, I see the good chute. The fear, the wind, the noise disappear. Replaced by pure peace. Silence. Quintessence. The worries of the world completely absent. What a gift. An extraordinary view of the aqua-blue Pacific Ocean flanked with the lush emerald-green Diamond Head peaks.

The crowd cheers as we glide through the grandstands, and we land. I even manage to avoid the $5 fine assessed for falling on my butt.

This incredible experience was topped off by the opportunity I had to share the message of the Folds of Honor Foundation. And thanks to great citizens such as my buddy Greg Nichols and my brothers-in-arms at Skydive Hawaii, we added a thousand more wingmen to the mission.

They say a picture is worth a thousand words. Well, I did an interview with my great friend Rich Lerner from Golf Channel and they showed some of the footage of the jump. As we watched I thought, "Now I know why birds sing."

The following day, Jacqy and I jumped together over the North Shore. "Gather ye rosebuds while ye may." "Carpe diem." Next item on the glorious bucket list of life?

Hanging out with Richard, Jacqy, and JC.

33.

BODY ARMOR

⭐

*Take care of your body, then the rest
will automatically become stronger.*

—CHUANG TZU

The fall leaves were bursting with color, and Jacqy and I were ready to seize the day as we embarked on the Marine Corps Marathon. The 26.2-mile course is an iconic blend of history and patriotism. We traversed our way through much of Washington, D.C., across the Potomac, through Georgetown, along the Mall, and around the Pentagon. Approaching mile 22, battling pain and exhaustion, the lactic acid shot fire throughout our legs, and our lungs struggled for air. Turning the corner, we labored to take one more stride and then suddenly our pain ceased. It had meaning as we gazed upon the thousands of mournful crosses in Arlington Cemetery. We felt honored that we could endure a small amount of physical pain on behalf of our nation's heroes. Jacqy, my sister Kate, and I were joined by PGA professionals and friends from across the country. Our team was running for the families that provide our freedom.

Pressing through mile 25, the U.S. Marine Corps War Memorial, also known as the Iwo Jima Memorial, came into view—the beautiful sculpture inspired by a photograph of the marines raising the flag atop the black volcanic ash-scarred earth of Mount Suribachi. The Memorial honors the over 26,000 casualties (nearly 7,000 killed) during one of the most significant battles of the Pacific in World War II. It was the perfect symbolism as we neared the end of our own personal battle. Running the Marine Corps marathon pushed us to the brink. It was a test. It was also an opportunity to down the intoxicating elixir of life. A portal to quintessence.

Like a marathon, each day life will test us physically, emotionally, and spirituality. Like soldiers preparing for battle, we must train and strengthen our minds and bodies to prepare for these tests. Conditioning our bodies improves every facet of our lives. It makes us happier, healthier, and more successful in our relationships and business.

Several years ago my path crossed with Lieutenant Colonel Lamont "Python" Cavanagh. Lamont is a sports medicine doctor and was also my flight surgeon. An elite group of Air Force doctors is charged with taking care of pilots. Flight surgeons are trained in all facets of the demanding realm that fighter pilots call "the office." There are few dominions in the world as unforgiving as flying at high altitudes, Mach 2 speeds, and the punishing force of 9 Gs. Dr. Cavanagh works with the pilots to ensure that they are prepared for the demanding nature of flying fighters. It's his job to make sure the pointy end of the spear stays razor sharp.

The foundation in the fighter-pilot nation, like life, starts with being fit in both mind and body. There is a reason it is the first ingredient in the body-mind-soul triad. If you take care of your body, it will take care of you. It is your most precious gift. Each day I take one hour to combine workouts and prayer. Fitness is an awesome force that has limitless power to change your life and help you realize your quintessence.

Crossing the marathon finish line.

34.

MAN'S SEARCH
FOR MEANING

I count him braver who overcomes his
desires than him who conquers his enemies;
for the hardest victory is over self.

—ARISTOTLE

We will all face challenges in life. Doctor Viktor E.
Frankl, a Holocaust survivor, teaches us that we have a
choice in our interpretation of any situation. How we choose
to look at life will have a profound impact on our happiness.
This excerpt from Frankl's book, *Man's Search for Meaning*,
is an extraordinary demonstration of the power of volition.

We must never forget that we may also find meaning
in life even when confronted with a hopeless situation,
when facing a fate that cannot be changed. For what
then matters is to bear witness to the uniquely human
potential at its best, which is to transform a personal
tragedy into a triumph, to turn one's predicament

225

into a human achievement. When we are no longer able to change a situation—just think of an incurable disease such as inoperable cancer—we are challenged to change ourselves.

Let me cite a clear-cut example: Once, an elderly general practitioner consulted me because of his severe depression. He could not overcome the loss of his wife who had died two years before and whom he had loved above all else. Now, how could I help him? What should I tell him? Well, I refrained from telling him anything but instead confronted him with the question, "What would have happened, Doctor, if you had died first, and your wife would have had to survive you?" "Oh," he said, "for her this would have been terrible; how she would have suffered!" Where-upon I replied, "You see, Doctor, such a suffering has been spared her, and it was you who have spared her this suffering—to be sure, at the price that now you have to survive and mourn her." He said no word but shook my hand and calmly left my office. In some way, suffering ceases to be suffering at the moment it finds a meaning, such as the meaning of a sacrifice.

35.

AN INVITATION

A consistent soul believes in destiny,
a capricious one in chance.

—BENJAMIN DISRAELI

President George W. Bush came across a story on the Folds of Honor Foundation and was inspired by our mission. As a result, I was invited by Defense Secretary Robert Gates on behalf of President Bush to attend his final address as commander-in-chief of the U.S. Armed Forces. My initial response? "Thank you sincerely for the invitation, but as my wife Jacqy is due with our fourth daughter in two weeks. I'm going to have to decline so I can stay close to home." I know I am an idiot, but in my defense I was under the impression that I was merely one of a thousand other people who were invited. Shortly after, Secretary Gates's assistant called to ask me to reconsider based on the fact that I was actually one of only a handful of people who had been singled out by President Bush. I quickly accepted the invitation before they changed their minds.

I was allowed to go in style to the President's final address. I flew to Washington, D.C., in an F-16. A comforting fact knowing that if Jacqy was to go into early labor I had a jet that could get me back home—fast!

My journey started on a Monday afternoon. I was scheduled to depart at 1400 and would be flying straight to Andrews Air Force Base. My jet had different plans.

When I strapped into the F-16, I hit Start 2. This fires both bottles of the jet fuel starter (JFS), which is a smaller motor that triggers the single Pratt & Whitney 229 engine of the F-16. As I selected Start 2, I was greeted by the sight and smell of fuel bubbling out of my left external tank. I was forced to shut down the jet and step to the spare jet. The military is in the business of preparing for the unexpected.

As the process of changing planes took about an hour, I found myself watching in frustration as the maintenance crew worked to upload the travel pod and get the jet ready for my departure. The travel pod connects under the wing on one of the armament stations. It fits a small suitcase and a set of golf clubs perfectly! My impatience quickly evaporated as my consciousness snapped into action. "What am I complaining about? I get to fly an F-16 to the capital city and see the President of the United States, albeit a little later than originally planned, but so what?" Furthermore, I realized that in 20 years I would likely be looking back and thinking, "If only I could relive that adventure."

A few minutes later I was climbing out of Tulsa with an unrestricted view of the world. As I leveled off at 28,000 feet, I checked my ETA into Andrews: a cool one hour and twenty-eight minutes. I was the benefactor of a 130-knot tailwind and was doing 720 miles per hour over the ground. For the next hour I snacked on a sandwich, enjoyed the speed, and reflected on life, which was indeed good.

As I approached Washington, D.C., I checked in with Potomac Approach and was cleared direct to Andrews. Due to the late takeoff, the time was about 1720, and a perfect twilight backlit the Washington Monument. I pushed over (changed radio frequencies) to Andrews Tower and was cleared to initial. In Air Force-speak, initial is the standard pattern that fighters fly. At 1,500 feet and 350 knots to the approach-end of the runway we make a a 3-5G break turn and come off the perch and land.

Approaching the airport from the West, I had run my before-landing checklist and was soaking up the view when I noticed a large airplane turning in front of me, lining up on the runway parallel to mine. I pushed up the throttle and soon I was flying in formation with the most famous plane in the world. I looked out the left side of the jet and there it was, "The Flying Oval Office" against the backdrop of the evening lights of our nation's capital. *What a great country!* We are all blessed by its traditions, commitment to democracy, and the opportunities it provides. Here I was, a runt kid from Stillwater, Oklahoma, in an F-16, flying in formation with President Bush's 747.

After landing, I shut down the jet and described what had happened to the maintenance crew at Andrews. "No big deal," they said. "We see that plane around here all the time."

That evening, while eating dinner alone, I said a prayer of thanks for the great day that I had just experienced, and I replayed the events in my mind.

"I almost missed it," I thought.

As I reflected on it, I realized that if my first jet had not had that fuel leak, I would not have been there at that precise moment...synchronicity.

I was up early the next morning to attend President Bush's address. I dusted off my formal Air Force Blues and grabbed a cab heading out to Fort Myer, the "old guard" of military bases, located in Arlington, Virginia. A grey blanket of cold and mist shrouded the area. As I peered out the cab window as I neared the fort, it quickly became clear why President Bush had picked this location: Fort Myer is surrounded by Arlington National Cemetery and flanked by the Iwo Jima Memorial.

I believe that all Americans should make a pilgrimage to this sacred place at least once in their lives. Although Washington, D.C., has many historic sites, nothing demonstrates our nation's sacrifice for our freedom more clearly than the eternally resting soldiers in Arlington National Cemetery.

As I jumped out of the cab, the scene I encountered was straight from a movie, complete with a security detail crawling around like ants. I was so excited that I forgot to put on my cover (flight cap). I reached down to retrieve it...*Oh no, I must have left it in the cab?* Thankfully due to inclement weather the ceremony had been moved indoors so I scurried inside...*safe*. Greeted by Secretary Gates's assistant, I was promptly shown to my seat alongside the joint chiefs of staff and behind First Lady Laura Bush, Vice President Dick Cheney, and General David Petraeus. It was amazing to be in the same room let alone sitting next to these patriots. My excitement was interrupted by an announcement, "Ladies and gentleman, we will be observing outdoor traditions for today's ceremony. Please don your covers." So there I sat, next to my military heroes without my cover. One of the generals quickly noticed the guy who did not look like everyone else; I was cringing on the inside. I reluctantly made eye contact. He winked, smiled, and shrugged his shoulders as if to say *we have all been there*.

President Bush's address was without question the most patriotic and formal ceremony I have ever attended. The honor guards from the U.S. Air Force, Army, Navy, Marines, and Coast Guard were all present, accompanied by the Army band.

The President spoke eloquently and with heartfelt emotion. He shared the battles he fought during his eight years as commander-in-chief. He discussed his years in office, the challenging situations he faced, and the difficult decisions he had to make. He certainly had been living in a realm between fear and faith.

The skies opened up as I left the historic address. With a smile on my face I reflected on the past two days, barely noticing the rain that was transforming my uniform from royal to navy blue.

Synchronicity would bring President Bush and myself back together. He has become a strong supporter of the Folds of Honor and our honorary chairman for Patriot Golf Day. It is one of the greatest honors in my life to have his support and friendship, and to play golf together. He is a true patriot and a very good golfer.

What an honor to meet President George W. Bush.

36.

THE RYDER CUP

★

There is but one cause of human failure.
And that is man's lack of faith in his true self.
—WILLIAM JAMES

Virtually every positive thing that has occurred in my life has some connection with golf. This tradition continued when Joe Steranka, CEO of PGA of America, asked me to introduce him for the March of Dimes award he was receiving in New York City. As a surprise, Ryder Cup Captain Corey Pavin and his wife Lisa came to celebrate Joe's honor. This chance meeting resulted in one of the most amazing opportunities of my life. Corey and Lisa invited me to give an inspirational talk to the Ryder Cup team in Wales. It was an incredible honor: I was the only outsider who would address the team. But I honestly wondered what I could share with Tiger Woods, Phil Michelson, and the other greatest golfers in the world. My typical Sunday was spent watching them on television, not inspiring them.

On Tuesday night before the Ryder Cup, I addressed the team, their wives, and the PGA of America officers. I shared

Joe Steranka, Jacqy, and Rickie.

stories about accountability and teamwork and about the honor of representing the United States of America. Corey specifically asked me to talk about trusting your teammate in pressure situations. From the outside it would seem that flying an F-16 is about as individualistic of an activity as there is. To the contrary, when we fly together, regardless of the number of airplanes in the sky, we share one spirit. We trust each other with our lives on every flight in combat and training.

Speaking to the team was one of the most special nights of my life. We all laughed and shed a few tears. On that night Jacqy and I made new friends. We gained a better understanding of who the greatest golfers in the world are outside the confines of the PGA Tour. To a man they impressed me with their passion for our country and the strength of their faith.

It was an incredible week to be a fan. Jacqy and I were inside the ropes and got to spend time with several of the team members. The Ryder Cup experience was filled with once-in-a-lifetime memories. But the most significant moment had nothing to do with the tournament. It was a powerful story of synchronicity that Tom Lehman shared with us.

In 1990, Tom and his wife Melissa departed Minneapolis en route to the Wichita Open. Tom was not a fully exempt player on the Ben Hogan Tour, thus he was not eligible to play every week. Tom and Melissa loaded Rachael, their four-month-old daughter, in the back seat and headed south. The roar of hot summer wind on Interstate 35 blasted through the windows of their air-conditionless 1985 graphite-grey GL40 Volvo. Tom had stopped to get the AC fixed a few weeks back before could not afford the $1,300 repair bill.

When Tom arrived in Wichita, he did not have a caddie. He asked around and ended up with a local high school wrestler on the bag. Mind you, this young kid knew nothing about golf. Over the next four days Tom and his bag carrier had a great run. Tom went on to win the tournament and received a $20,000 check, by far the biggest payday of his career to that point. And it could not have come at a more opportune time. The Lehmans were living day to day; the money was a precious gift.

When Tom finished the tournament, he realized that he was obligated to pay his caddie. The typical fee for a caddie on the tour is 10 percent of the winnings. Tom struggled because his young caddie did nothing other than carry the bag. He did not give a yardage, read a putt, or offer any advice. It was evident that he did not provide the service that warranted a $2,000 paycheck.

Tom asked his wife Melissa about it, and her response was to follow his heart. Even though the Lehmans desperately needed the money, Tom decided the right thing to do was to err on the side of generosity. He paid his caddie the $2,000.

Several months later, Tom received a letter in the mail from his young caddie. He shared that he was from a large family and his dad had abandoned them, leaving only his mom to raise the kids. She was working several jobs just to make ends meet. Under these stressful living conditions he had found his way into trouble with drugs and alcohol. But he understood that he had to change his life and had recently found the Lord. He found a purpose in wrestling and direction through the Fellowship of Christian Athletes. With his life back on track, he dreamed of going to college at a local Bible school. Despite his exceptional efforts, his mom did not have the funds to send him to school. The tuition was exactly $2,000. With Tom's check the young caddie would be able to attend college.

Tom summed up the experience this way: "I was so humbled when I received his letter. I was humbled to think that God had chosen me to help change this young man's life. That I fit in the bigger picture of life. It was a powerful life lesson about focusing on others and not on yourself. I was so encouraged because I had done the right thing and witnessed the effects of my decision. I was at peace walking with the Lord. I was thankful that I was part of His plan."

It was obvious to Jacqy and me that this was yet another demonstration of synchronicity, integrity, and the divine mixture of life. If we don't commit to using our time and talents to impact the world, then why are we here?

I don't think it is a coincidence at all that Tom went on to have an incredible career. He won the 1996 British Open, earned over $20,000,000, and has stayed true to his quintessence, raising millions for charity. In life when you do good things, good things happen.

I presented the Ryder Cup team with
authentic A2 aviator jackets.

37.

BETWEEN FEAR
AND FAITH

*Faith is to believe what you do not yet see;
the reward for this faith is to see
what you believe.*

—SAINT AUGUSTINE

Edwards Air Force Base in California is home to the Air Force Flight Test Center. The base encompasses more than 300,000 acres and features a couple of dried-out lakebeds that provide plenty of contingency space. Originally known as Muroc Army Air Field, it is the spot from where one of my personal heroes, Chuck Yeager, made his historic flight traveling faster than sound.

Most F-16 pilots will visit this vast research environment once in their careers. The mission is to take up the jet, intentionally send it out of control, and then recover it. The purpose behind these exercises is to determine just how far you can push the envelope and to prove to yourself that you can recover when you go too far.

Our lives are no different. We must go beyond our limits to know where those limits are. Only then can we grow. We will never achieve quintessence unless we venture into the realm between fear and faith. We must commit to pushing ourselves physically, emotionally, and spiritually in the pursuit of finding out why we are here.

Don't waste another moment. That feeling of discontent in your soul is God calling you to action. Figure out what you love to do and start doing it. Make a commitment to yourself and summon the courage to take whatever action is necessary. It's natural to fear failure and its companions, pain, ridicule, and suffering. It's natural to be scared of losing what you have accumulated. But don't let the storms created in your mind keep you from taking the great voyage of life. Most of us spend our lives bound by the fear of storms that never happen. Fear is prevalent in everyone's life. Courage is taking action despite fear. Those rare individuals who embrace their life's calling have the faith to raise their sails and depart the safe harbors for the open waters.

When you pursue quintessence, you will be rewarded in unimaginable ways. You will discover that you are capable of doing things you never dreamed possible. You will encounter amazing people and accumulate an extraordinary bucket of life experiences. Your spirit will grow as a result of your actions.

Just remember that there are no shortcuts to quintessence, but don't worry because faith will be your shield. Fitness will be your body armor, persistence your ally.

When you chase those big dreams, be ready to experience big failures. Failure is part of our divine path. Success and failure are equally important parts of our journey, both characters in life's unique story. Each is placed in our lives to help us grow and become better people. The sweetness of victory would not exist without the bitterness of defeat; without failure there would be no success. True failure occurs only when we fail to grow and learn from our mistakes and experiences. When you stumble, smile, evaluate, and press on. In the end, it is not about what you accomplish but rather what you overcome.

My parents taught me that I was obligated to utilize my time and my talents. They reminded me that my blessings were not to be wasted. I firmly believe that we will be judged not by what we have attained but rather what we have done for others. Love yourself and the people in your life. Forgive those who have done you wrong. Commit to a cause bigger than yourself. Challenge yourself to get a little better each day.

God gave us free will, but we have to use it. Our choices will define us. They become our life's story. Harness the power of volition. There is no greater tragedy than letting life simply run its course. Those timid souls who have never ventured into the realm between fear and faith will die in deep regret.

Whether it was hitting a little white ball or striking a target on the ground from 30,000 feet, I have spent my life in the realm between fear and faith. It is there that I discovered quintessence. Through testing, challenging, and living on the outer edges of life I have developed a set of maxims. It is a constant struggle to balance them and hold myself accountable. I hope these maxims will help set you on a path to quintessence. Commit to pursuing your quintessence. Push yourself physically, emotionally, and spiritually each day.

Every morning I wake my girls with the same ritual. "What is today?"

A little sleepy voice replies, "The greatest day of my life."

"Why?" I ask.

"Because it's the only one we have."

Godspeed on your journey,

38.

MAXIMS OF
A PATRIOT

- Quintessence: The purest and most concentrated essence of you. Commit to living a life focused on discovering your essence.

- Faith: Recognize and embrace the synchronicity in your life.

- Prayer: Dedicate time each day to pray, and pray deeply. Prayer is a powerful portal to quintessence.

- Attitude: Positive thoughts will create a positive life force in your world.

- Fitness: Exercise your mind and body every day or you may lose them. Fulfillment and productivity are directly proportional to our level of wellness.

- Open heart and open mind...Learn from the people and experiences in your life.

- Passion: Figure out what you love to do and do it every day.

- Courage: Take action and make immediate change. Bravery is taking that first step despite fear.

- Persistence and tenacity: Overcome obstacles and stay positive. Without failure there would be no success. Life is about what we overcome, not what we achieve.

- Commitment: Set goals and never quit. Get a little better each day.

- Accountability: Expect it first from yourself and then from others.

- Trust: Have trust in the universe, and you will be rewarded.

- Integrity: It is doing the right thing when no one is looking.

- Service and sacrifice: We're called to make the world a better place. You will discover that when you reach out to help someone, you are actually the one being helped. In the end we will be judged not by what we have accomplished for ourselves but by what we have done for others.

- Forgiveness: That which offers us a portal to heal the spirit.

- Compassion: Love yourself and others.

- Gratitude: Say *thank you*. Our lives are the culmination of the opportunities we have been given.

Say thank you by passing on an opportunity to someone else.

- Volition: Choose to make your life extraordinary.

EPILOGUE

THE HALF
WHO STAYED

★

Happiness is the meaning and the purpose of life,
the whole aim and end of human existence.

—ARISTOTLE

December 7, 1941—a date which will live in infamy—
the United States of America was suddenly and
deliberately attacked by naval and air forces of the Empire
of Japan. Joint Base Pearl Harbor Hickam stands today as
a symbol of American pride and resiliency. The scars left
from strafing runs by Japanese Zeros are still visible on
many buildings. They were left intentionally unrepaired as a
constant reminder to remain vigilant. Freedom is not free.

It was a tranquil morning. The sun rays glistened over
the emerald-green mountains of Oahu. At just past 0800,
our four-ship of F-16s was cleared for takeoff on the reef
runway—a stark contrast to the events that had taken place
57 years earlier, at 0748 to be exact.

As I pulled on the runway, I checked the engine and lifted the throttle over the detent. The F-16's afterburner unleashed 29,000 pounds of thrust. The raw speed pushed me back against the seat. Racing down the runway, I slowly pulled back on the stick and soon was where I was born to be—flying.

Released from the burden of gravity, I made an immediate 5-G turn to avoid giving a window-shaking wake-up call to the tourists sleeping soundly in the hotels lining Waikiki Beach. My right 270 turn took me out over the Pacific and then directly up Pearl Harbor. On the climb I rolled the Viper over and witnessed one of the most patriotic scenes of my entire life. I looked down through the clear canopy with emotional admiration at the USS Arizona. The leaking oil, representing the tears of men entombed in her hull, was shimmering on the water. It was a haunting reminder that we must never forget those who have paid the ultimate price for our freedom. It is our duty to honor their sacrifice and preserve the American way of life. The message delivered by Franklin D. Roosevelt following the attack heard 'round the world remains as relevant as it was that stoic December day: *Defeat is not an option.*

In that same American spirit of 1941, we must not fail to answer the call of duty. Though the enemy is different, once again the United States of America is under attack. President Kennedy captured it best with his infamous call to action: "Ask not what your country can do for you, but rather what you can do for your country." We are called as patriots to give back to the United States of America.

While we will never be able to fully erase the pain or reverse the loss that every combat casualty causes, we can express our gratitude for every sacrifice. We can heighten awareness, spread the message, and remind people of all the things that servicemen and -women do for our country. It is our duty, as Americans, to educate the legacy of each soldier killed or wounded in the line of duty.

Over 4,800 U.S. military members have died and more than 33,500 have been wounded in Iraq and Afghanistan. The U.S. Department of Veterans Affairs estimates that 1,000,000 spouses and kids have had a family member wounded or killed in Iraq or Afghanistan. Approximately 87 percent of these dependents do not qualify for any federal education assistance.

As of September of 2014, through Patriot Golf Day and the Folds of Honor Foundation, we had raised over $40 million to help over 7,500 dependents in all 50 states pursue

Spending time with recipients is the highlight of my work at Folds of Honor.

the dream of an education. I express my heartfelt appreciation to all who have stepped up in support of our cause. We couldn't have done it without you, but we need even more wingmen to carry out this mission.

Earlier I shared with you a story about volition. I am asking you to exercise that powerful gift, that powerful ally, the power to choose. I am asking you to choose to act, choose to be a patriot, and choose to join me and the half who stayed aboard United Flight 664.

FOLDS *of* HONOR

www.foldsofhonor.org

Our military families need your help on this mission. Become a wingman!

1. Purchase *A Patriot's Calling*. $1 from each book sale is donated to the Folds of Honor Foundation and will change a life.* Visit www.patriotscalling.com to purchase.

2. Share *A Patriot's Calling* with your family and friends. Ask your local library to carry the book.

3. Visit www.foldsofhonor.org and make a donation.

4. Enlist as a wingman on www.foldsofhonor.org and pass on the website to everyone you know.

5. Play in Patriot Golf Day over Labor Day weekend. Make sure that courses in your local area are signed up. www.patriotgolfday.com

6. Host an event for the Folds of Honor Foundation. Visit www.foldsofhonor.org to find out more information.

7. Join The Patriot as a national member and fund a scholarship. www.patriotgolfclub.com

*$1.00 from each book sale after the publishing cost has been recuperated.

ACKNOWLEDGMENTS

Socrates called his fellow man to employ time improving ourselves by other men's writings, so that we shall gain easily what others have labored hard to discover.

My office shelves bear proof of my constant search for enlightenment. Well-worn, dusty books tower from the floor to the ceiling. But on the nightstand my constant companions rest—the Bible, *The Power of Now, The Alchemist, The World's Greatest Salesman,* and *Man's Search for Meaning*—always ready at the end of a hard day to offer me hope and guidance. They have become part of who I am, and their inspiration rushes through the pages of *A Patriot's Calling.*

To Paul Brothers, Roger Chasteen, Jeff Smith, and Dad for helping bring this book to life.

BIBLIOGRAPHY

Eye of the Viper, The Making of an F-16 Pilot, Peter Aleshire, The Lyons Press 2005

The Alchemist, by Paulo Coelho, Harper Collins 1993

The World's Greatest Salesman, by OG Mandino, MJF Books, 1968

When War Played Through, by John Strege, Penguin Books, 2005

Man's Search for Meaning, Victor E. Frankl, Beacon Press, 1959

www.spiritandflesh.com/physics_Meek_WIMPS_dark_matter_quintessence_Pentecost.ht

www.tabbykatus.tripod.com/id5.html

www.tabbykatus.tripod.com/id5.html My Quiet Hero Website

Scott Thomas article from www.mysanantonio.com/sports/article/Scott-Thomas-Ejecting-out-of-a-flaming-fighter-1379132.php#page1

Special Thanks

Bushnell

Titleist

Ralph Lauren

It would be an honor to share my message of hope, inspiration, patriotism and living in a realm between fear and faith. I have been blessed to share my stories with US Ryder Cup Team, PGA professionals, and Fortune 500 companies-a few include Anheuser Bush, Wells-Fargo, and Northwestern Mutual. I am available for a limited amount of speaking engagements. Please direct inquiries to the Washington Speakers Bureau info@washingtonspeakers.com or call 703-684-0555.

ABOUT THE AUTHOR

Major Dan "Noonan" Rooney has flown his F-16 on three tours of duty in Iraq. He is retired and is currently on Inactive Ready Reserve in the Air National Guard. He is a PGA golf professional, motivational speaker, founder of The Patriot Golf Club, and the founder and President of the Folds of Honor Foundation. The Folds of Honor has raised millions and awarded over 2,600 educational scholarships for the families of fallen and disabled veterans. He has been awarded the Air National Guard's Distinguished Service Medal, Air Force Combat Air Medal, Ellis Island Medal of Honor, and PGA of America's first Patriot Award. He was given the Call to Service award by President George W. Bush and was named one *People* magazine's Heroes of the Year and ABC World News's Persons of the Year. In A Patriot's Calling, he inspires us to discover our essence and give back to America.

Spain

Seville, Spain

EUROPE

AFRICA

Noonan's Exploration of Life